Signs of Writing

Signs of Writing

Roy Harris

London and New York

First published 1995
by Routledge
11 New Fetter Lane, London EC4P 4EE

Simultaneously published in the USA and Canada
by Routledge
29 West 35th Street, New York, NY 10001

© 1995 Roy Harris

Typeset in Baskerville by
Ponting–Green Publishing Services, Chesham, Bucks
Printed and bound in Great Britain by
Biddles Ltd, Guildford and King's Lynn

British Library Cataloguing in Publication Data
A catalogue record for this book is available from the
British Library

Library of Congress Cataloguing in Publication Data
A catalogue record for this book has been requested

ISBN 0–415–10088–7

Contents

Acknowledgements

The author and publisher gratefully acknowledge the following sources of illustrations: Figs 1.1, 1.2 and 1.3 (G.L. Trager, 'Writing and writing systems', *Current Trends in Linguistics*, Vol. 12, ed. T.A. Sebeok, The Hague/Paris: Mouton, 1974, pp. 378–9); Fig. 9.1 (S.V. Beyer, *The Classical Tibetan Language*, Albany: State University of New York Press, 1992, p. 52); Fig. 10.1 (E.B. Tylor, *Anthropology*, London: Macmillan, 1881, Ch. VII); Fig. 13.2 (E. Gower, 'Bar codes', *Schools Mathematics Project News*, No. 19, 25 March 1983); Fig. 15.1 (E.H. Antonsen, 'The runes: the earliest Germanic writing system', *The Origins of Writing*, ed. W.M. Senner, Lincoln/London: University of Nebraska Press, p. 142); Fig. 17.1 (Brasserie Balzar, Paris); Fig. 17.2 (H. Franke, 'Chinese patterned texts', *Visible Language*, xx, 1, 1986, p. 100); Fig. 18.1 (M.D. Coe, *Breaking the Maya Code*, New York: Thames & Hudson, 1992, p. 253); Fig. 19.1 (H. Sottas and E. Drioton, *Introduction à l'étude des hiéroglyphes*, Paris: Geuthner, 1991, p. 56); Fig. 20.2 (M.A. Powell, Jr, 'The origin of the sexagesimal system: the interaction of language and writing', *Visible Language*, vi, 1 1972, p. 16); Fig. 20.3 (J.C.P. Miller and F.C. Powell, *The Cambridge Elementary Mathematical Tables*, Cambridge: Cambridge University Press, 1965, p. 28); Fig. 20.4 (C.B. Boyer, *A History of Mathematics*, 2nd edn, New York: Wiley, 1991, p. 216); Fig. 20.5 (J. Needham, *Science and Civilization in China*, Vol. 3, Cambridge: Cambridge University Press, 1959, p. 135); Fig. 21.1 (Sirdar PLC, Wakefield); Figs 21.2, 21.3 and 21.4 (V. Silvester, *Modern Ballroom Dancing*, rev. edn, North Pomfret: Trafalgar Square, 1993, p. 45, p. 59); Fig. 21.5 (B. Blistène *et al.*, *L'Ecriture de la danse*, Paris: Bibliothèque-Musée de l'Opéra, 1993, p. 14); Fig. 21.6 (D. Diringer, *The Alphabet*, 2nd edn, London: Hutchinson, 1949, p. 78); Fig. 21.7 (AT&T Inc., New Jersey); Figs 21.8 and 21.9 (A. Hutchinson, *Labanotation*, 3rd edn rev., New York: Routledge Theatre Arts, 1977, p. 26, p. 433); Fig. 21.10 (A.J. Marett, 'Tunes notated in flute-tablature from a Japanese source of the tenth century', *Musica Asiatica*, i, 1977, p. 26); Appendix D Fig. 1 (A. Cavanagh, *Lettering and Alphabets*, New York: Dover, 1955, p. 24); Plate 1 (Bibliothèque municipale, Dijon, Ms. 168, f.4 verso: Association des amis de la bibliothèque municipale de Dijon and Cliché Minirel, Quetigny);

Plate 7 (A.A. Cohen, *Dada. The Avant-Garde in Print 3*, New York: Matthews, 1981); Plate 9 (ADAGP and Flammarion, Paris); Plate 11 (Makers of Ah-So sauce); Plate 12 (W.A. Smalley, C.K. Vang and G.Y. Yang, *Mother of Writing, The Origin and Development of a Hmong Messianic Script*, Chicago: University of Chicago Press, 1990, p. 98); Plate 13 (W.M. Wrigley Jr Co., Chicago); Plate 16 (*Boston Globe*, 9 December 1993); Plate 18 (British Museum); Plate 19 (Nancy Trueworthy and Coastal Exposures Inc., Maine).

The author would also like to thank Anthony Barrand and Beth Soll for answering questions about dance notation, and students at Boston University who attended a series of lectures on *Writing and Civilization* in 1994 for helpful comments on many points.

Introduction

It is a striking paradox that the Western academic tradition, which has relied so extensively on writing – as opposed to oral transmission – for its very existence, has so far produced no comprehensive theory of writing itself. This is not to say that important questions about writing have not been raised and debated. But they have usually been raised as side-issues relevant to other concerns rather than as a coherent set of questions in their own right.

Realizing this, I.J. Gelb some forty years ago set out to 'lay a foundation for a new science of writing'. For this new science he proposed the name *grammatology*.[1]

Why was grammatology needed? While recognizing that much of value had been published about writing, Gelb pointed out that all the available books on the subject were 'characterized by a historical–descriptive treatment'.[2] But, as he rightly observed, 'a simple narrative approach to a subject does not make it into a science'.[3]

Unfortunately, Gelb's attempt to lay the foundation for his 'new science' was a failure, as is now generally recognized. But it was a failure from which important lessons can be learnt.

First, Gelb failed because his 'foundation' turned out to be no more than a classification of writing systems, and not a particularly original one. In fact, the 'systematic typology'[4] he proposed was simply an updated version of views which had been current for the previous two hundred years among European scholars who had studied the differences between the major writing systems of the world. As Derrida remarked, 'in spite of a concern for systematic or simplified classification, and in spite of the controversial hypotheses on the monogenesis or polygenesis of scripts, this book follows the classical model of histories of writing'.[5] What Gelb evidently failed to

---

1 I.J. Gelb, *A Study of Writing* (Chicago: University of Chicago Press, 1952; rev. edn 1963).
2 *Ibid.*, p. 23.
3 *Ibid.*, p. 23.
4 *Ibid.*, p. 23.
5 J. Derrida, *Of Grammatology*, trans. G.C. Spivak (Baltimore: Johns Hopkins University Press, 1974), p. 323, n. 4.

realize was that a typology, however neat it may be and however impeccable its historical credentials, is only as good as the theoretical assumptions underlying it. These assumptions Gelb did not investigate, much less question. Thus his grammatology appeared to be founded less on an analysis of writing itself than upon a conspectus of how European scholars had traditionally classified its better-known varieties.

Second, Gelb's view of a 'science' of writing was an evolutionary view. His new science was one which would seek to 'establish general principles governing the use and evolution of writing'.[6] He took it for granted that writing had 'evolved' and that evolution meant improvement. Thus it is not surprising that his survey of writing systems presented the history of mankind's experiments with written communication as a slow progress from 'primitive' to more advanced forms, beginning with crude pictography and culminating eventually in the kind of script to which European academics were themselves most accustomed – namely, alphabetic writing. Nor did he hesitate to associate 'primitive' forms of writing with 'primitive' peoples, and even insisted on the term *primitive*.[7]

Third, Gelb's 'new science' failed unaccountably to take much notice of the existence of other forms of writing than those that can be used to record human speech. Such fields as mathematical and musical notation receive scant attention. This is all the more curious in that Gelb's definition of writing (*a system of human intercommunication by means of conventional visible marks*)[8] was so broad as to take in *prima facie* a variety of signs not usually regarded as falling under the designation *writing* at all.

Finally, if the view of writing as a form of communication is to be taken seriously, as Gelb's own definition suggests, then it becomes important to ensure that what is proposed as a foundation for a science of writing is itself soundly based upon a more general theory of human communication. But no such theory is in fact propounded by Gelb, beyond vague references to the 'expression' of ideas and the communication of 'thoughts' and 'feelings'.

In short, Gelb's proposed foundation of grammatology begs the very questions that are most controversial in any attempt to establish a broad theoretical basis for the study of writing.

In fairness to Gelb, it should be pointed out that in 1952 the potential academic audience for any 'science of writing' was very small. It was in practice limited to those scholars who were primarily concerned in one way

---

6 Gelb, *A Study of Writing*, p. v.
7 *Ibid.*, p. 273 n42.
8 *Ibid.*, p. 12. A quarter of a century later, Gelb proposed a somewhat different definition: 'Writing in its broadest sense is a recording system or device by means of conventional markings or shapes or color of objects, achieved by the motor action of the hand and received visually by another' (I.J. Gelb, 'Principles of writing systems within the frame of visual communication', in P.A. Kolers, M.E. Wrolstad and H. Bouma (eds), *Processing of Visible Language*, vol. 2 (New York: Plenum, 1980), p. 22.)

or another with the study of ancient civilizations (as Gelb himself was). Among linguists there reigned a virtually unanimous consensus that the study of writing as such did *not* fall within their field, even though linguists might sometimes – unfortunately – be forced to use written evidence in the course of their investigations.[9] As Basso observes:

> writing was consigned to a position of decidedly minor importance. Textbooks continued to include brief chapters on the subject, but this was to emphasize that writing and language were entirely distinct and that the former had no place within the domain of modern linguistics.[10]

Since the original publication of Gelb's book, the situation has changed radically in a number of ways. First, the development of postmodernist critical theory has re-examined the theoretical status of writing and the written text in ways never before explored in the Western tradition. Second, Gelb was expounding views uninfluenced by more recent controversies concerning the distinction between 'orality' and 'literacy' and the thesis that 'writing restructures thought'. Third, the last few decades have seen a noticeable increase in the number of linguists willing to consider writing as a form of language in its own right. Fourth, in 1952 it was not yet apparent to most people how significantly the domain of writing was to be extended by computer technology.

For all these reasons, it is no longer possible to take Gelb's ambitious pioneering work even as a point of departure. What a general theory of writing requires today is a framework which, above all, does not *prejudge* the relations between writing and other forms of communication; it must be a framework which leaves these relations open to empirical investigation, while at the same time offering a coherent rationale underlying the conduct of such enquiries.

The essential business of the theorist is to open up new avenues of understanding, rather than to summarize and systematize old accumulations of (supposedly established) facts. Theorizing involves showing how different questions may be interrelated and proposing a structure within which this interrelationship can be clearly exhibited. Without such a structure there can be no *theory* of writing, but only a series of *ad hoc* answers to *ad hoc* questions. In order to have the basis for a theory, it is necessary to identify a point of view which will permit the investigator to tackle a whole range of questions from a single perspective; that is, to approach them in a consistent and systematic manner and to offer answers that are not only coherent in themselves but rationally connected. Thus, for example, a theory of writing should allow such questions as 'How does writing

---

9 A notable exception is the work of Josef Vachek.
10 K.H. Basso, 'The ethnography of writing', in R. Bauman and J. Sherzer (eds), *Explorations in the Ethnography of Speaking* (Cambridge: Cambridge University Press, 1974), pp. 425–32.

originate?', 'What types of writing systems are there?' and 'Is writing linear or non-linear?' to be seen as related facets of the same enquiry and not as separate, self-contained issues. To provide a theoretical framework of this kind is the sole objective of the present book.[11]

Unlike Gelb's grammatology, this framework has an internal logic. It (i) begins by specifying which view of human communication will be adopted, (ii) states the relevant constraints within which writing may be identified as a form of communication, and (iii) shows how varying combinations of factors correlate with actual and possible forms of writing. Thus conclusions reached under (iii) must answer to criteria stated in accordance with (ii), which in turn will conform to the perspective identified under (i). Adopting such a framework yields the bonus of allowing different theories of writing to be compared one with another in a quite exact way, depending on the varying positions the theorists take with respect to (i), (ii) and (iii).

A preliminary outline of how this structure will be applied in the following chapters may be given as follows.

(i)   The view of human communication adopted here is integrational as opposed to telementational. That is to say, communication is envisaged not as a process of transferring thoughts or messages from one individual mind to another, but as consisting in the contextualized integration of human activities by means of signs.

(ii) The relevant constraints on human communication are taken to be (a) biomechanical, (b) macrosocial and (c) circumstantial. Biomechanical factors relate to the physiological and psychological capacities of the human organism. Macrosocial factors relate to the cultural practices and institutions established in particular communities. Circumstantial factors proper relate to the context of communication and the actual activities involved.

(iii) Variation of biomechanical, macrosocial and circumstantial para-meters will be shown to correspond to characteristic forms of writing (e.g. glottic, mathematical, musical) and to different ways of organizing text.

Operating within a framework of this type allows typologies of writing to emerge from systematic analysis. An *a priori* typology does not, as in Gelb's theory of writing, dictate everything else.

Thus what is proposed here is to treat writing as a function of the versatile human capacity for sign-making. The study attempts to analyse the basic

---

11   Thus it differs in a number of respects from most general books about writing that are still in print. It is not a world survey of the many different kinds of scripts used at various times and places. Nor does it trace the history of particular writing systems. The social and educational implications of literacy, important though these have been and still are, are not its concern either.

principles operative in this uniquely complex form of communication, irrespective of whether the text produced is a Shakespeare sonnet, the score of Beethoven's Fifth Symphony, a signature on a cheque or the label on merchandise in a supermarket.

* * *

Such a study may be termed 'semiological' in the broadest sense and thus takes its place in a certain academic tradition.

The semiological approach to writing was first proposed in the early years of the present century by Ferdinand de Saussure, the founder of modern structuralism.[12] Although his view of language was original and revolutionary, Saussure's view of writing, by contrast, was deeply traditional, since for his purposes writing was primarily of interest as a *document de langue*. As a result, the potential inherent in applying semiological analysis to writing remained unexploited.[13]

C.S. Peirce, who initiated a different approach to the study of signs, used one form of writing – the printed word – as a basis for his influential distinction between *type* and *token*, a distinction later borrowed by linguists in their attempts to systematize the description of speech.[14] But Peirce, like Saussure, while taking writing for granted, failed to develop an analysis of the written sign itself.

The present study takes up the semiology of writing at the point where Saussure and Peirce left it, and proposes a radical alternative – the integrationist alternative – based on premises which are different from those adopted by Saussure, Peirce or any of their successors.

For the integrationist the fact, long recognized by psychologists, that 'the process of writing is an integration of skills'[15] is simply one aspect of a more general truth about human communication. Communication itself, whatever form it takes, is an integration of activities, rather than a separate form of activity carried out in addition to others; and the product of that integration, as well as its enabling mechanism, is the sign.

In the case of writing, the activities that have to be integrated for communication to take place are designated globally, but vaguely, by the traditional terms *writing* and *reading*. Biomechanically, the two are independent (as is shown by the possibility of being able to read without being

---

12 Ferdinand de Saussure, *Cours de linguistique générale*, 2nd edn (Paris: Payot, 1922).
13 It is interesting to note that in *A Study of Writing* Gelb never once refers to Saussure, even though Gelb's typology of scripts and his view of the relationship between writing and speech are essentially the same as those Saussure had advanced a quarter of a century previously.
14 *The Collected Papers of Charles Sanders Peirce*, vols I–VI, ed. C. Hartshorne and P. Weiss (Cambridge, Mass.: Harvard University Press, 1931–5); vols VII–VIII, ed. A. Burks (Cambridge, Mass.: Harvard University Press, 1958).
15 M. Martlew, 'The development of writing: communication and cognition'. In F. Coulmas and K. Ehlich (eds), *Writing in Focus* (Berlin, New York and Amsterdam: Mouton, 1983), pp. 257–75.

able to write); but as constituents of the process of communication they are interdependent, i.e. necessarily integrated. In other words, whatever can in principle be written must in principle be readable. The two types of activity are linked semiologically by a relationship of reciprocal pre-supposition.

An integrational approach to writing rests upon this single premiss and on the development of its theoretical implications.

Self-evidently true as the basic premiss may seem, the fact remains that no semiological study has hitherto examined the consequences that may be drawn from it as a foundation for the study of writing. Integrational phenomena are structured in such a way that the possibility of a later operation depends on the execution of an earlier operation, which in turn derives its significance from the anticipation of that possibility.

Many human endeavours are structured in this way, and writing very obviously so. Perhaps, indeed, the very perspicuousness of the fact has led to its neglect as a potential basis for the analysis of writing. Nor should this strike anyone as surprising. For the obviousness of a truth bears no relation at all to the complexity of recognizing what follows from it. The present study of writing makes no claim to have exhausted all the implications of the integrational premiss on which it is based.

It is not for the semiologist to usurp the psychologist's role and claim to explain exactly how the complex co-ordination of motor capacities, per-ceptions and stores of knowledge is accomplished in writing or any other form of communication. That such an integration is necessary and is achieved *somehow* the semiologist may take for granted. The product of that integration, the sign, poses problems which in any case extend beyond the province of psychology as such. These problems can in no way be solved or even illuminated by empirical psychological research (as both Saussure and Peirce clearly saw), for signs have their own logic, and it is this logic which constitutes the domain of semiology.

In one important respect, moreover, the psychologist's viewpoint is almost diametrically opposed to the semiologist's. In reading through the seemingly endless stream of publications by psychologists on reading and writing, a semiologist cannot fail to be struck not only by the crude ethnocentricity of much that appears on this subject, but also by the extent to which the psychologist is willing to treat the sign as something externally given, an object already provided by society for the learner to 'acquire' and utilize. In spite of all the talk of 'cognitive' abilities, it is as if learning to read and write were in the end on a par with learning how to use a knife and fork. There is no analysis of the sign itself, even though it is assumed that the sign is somehow the linchpin of the whole communicational enterprise.

For the semiologist, the written sign is a rather exceptional case in the domain of signs, inasmuch as its development has given rise to such a range of specialized tools and techniques. Writing with a reed stylus on wet clay is manifestly such a different enterprise from operating a modern printing press that it becomes legitimate to ask: is there any semiological unity underlying this diversity? This is one of the questions the present study attempts to answer.

From an integrational point of view, the mistake embodied in the traditional Western view of writing is plain: it confuses the function of the written sign with just one of its possible uses. An integrational semiology must show how and why the signs of writing function in a way that is basically different from the signs of speech, even when the purpose of the written text is to record a spoken message. It must also provide answers to the theoretical problems involved in distinguishing writing from gesture as well as from drawing, painting and other forms of graphic expression.

The integrationist, as noted above, explains the written sign by reference to the contextualized integration of the activities of writing and reading. But these activities in turn are seen by the integrationist as depending on the biomechanical capacities of the human body and the human mind. Furthermore, they are activities which would not exist were it not for their relevance to other patterns of activity in the community at large. In the domain of writing, therefore, an integrational analysis will take into account both biomechanical and macrosocial factors as pertinent to any comprehensive analysis. What all this adds up to is a reversal of the priorities tacitly accepted in many discussions of writing. Instead of treating writing and reading as activities made possible by the prior existence of written signs, written signs are treated as the communicational products of writing and reading.

Looking at writing in this perspective leads to the elaboration of concepts and distinctions which go considerably beyond those recognized in traditional accounts of writing: for example, the integrationist is led to recognize the importance of the concept of 'graphic space' and the distinctions between 'script' and 'notation', and between 'internal' and 'external' syntagmatics. Some of these have been discussed in earlier publications by the present writer.[16] Here they are presented as part of a more comprehensive theoretical framework.

No single book can attempt to tackle every question about writing. The topics discussed in Parts II, III and IV are intended simply as illustrations of how some major features of writing can be dealt with on an integrational basis and to suggest by implication how the approach might be taken further. What I have not attempted to do is pursue in detail the topics thus opened up. Should this give rise to criticisms that not enough has been said about any of them, the reply is that this was never the object of the exercise.

16   In particular, *The Origin of Writing* (London: Duckworth, 1986) and *La Sémiologie de l'écriture* (Paris: CNRS, 1994).

The present purpose is to sketch a theoretical framework which would make it possible to say more (i.e. more than can be said within the conceptual limits imposed by traditional Western accounts of writing).

The picture of writing which emerges from integrational analysis is one which may appear initially disconcerting. It challenges certain preconceptions which have been long entrenched in educational practices and accepted as gospel by many linguistic theorists of the past hundred years. It may even appear to introduce a new and unfamiliar concept of writing itself. Nevertheless, it is a picture that will be found to correspond more convincingly than any other not only to our everyday experience as writers and readers but also to possibilities for the future development of writing which are only just beginning to be explored.

Part I

A theory of writing

Chapter 1

Perspectives on writing

Writing is a strange invention.
Claude Lévi-Strauss

Whether writing was invented or merely evolved is an issue that may be debated.[1] But if writing was an invention, then, as Lévi-Strauss remarks, it is a strange one. Some inventions are doubtless stranger than others, but the strangest must be those which baffle their inventors. Into this class falls writing. Long familiarity with the practices and applications of writing does not immediately yield an understanding of what it is that has been invented.

What is not open to doubt, however, is that *writing systems* may be invented. Human beings have proved adept at inventing them for a great variety of purposes. Writing makes it possible to record business transactions, to set down stories and musical compositions, to do complex mathematical calculations, to choreograph dances, to keep calendars and accounts, and to deal with information of many different kinds. But it is perfectly possible to devise and use a system of writing for some particular purpose without having any understanding of the basic principles underlying writing as such. This should no more surprise us than the fact that it is possible to invent many kinds of simple machine without any understanding of the basic principles of mechanics. Nevertheless, any machine that works must conform to those principles. Similarly, any writing system that works must be based on certain general principles, even though it may not be clear to those who set up or use the system what these basic principles are.

In other words, understanding what writing makes possible is not at all the same thing as understanding what makes writing possible. The latter is the primary focus of attention in the present study.

The question of what makes writing possible is first and foremost the concern of the semiologist. Inasmuch as written signs constitute one

---

1 R. Harris, *The Origin of Writing* (London: Duckworth, 1986), Ch. 3; J.S. Pettersson, *Critique of Evolutionary Accounts of Writing* (RUUL no. 21), (Uppsala: Department of Linguistics, Uppsala University, 1991).

important subclass of the totality of signs involved in human communication, any general theory of signs must apply to the signs of writing. In order to show what makes writing possible, the semiologist has to make explicit the basic semiological principles to which written texts conform.

However, the study of writing poses an initial conceptual problem which it would be foolish to ignore or to attempt to brush aside. It is a problem that arises in part from the fact that the term *writing* has come to be applied to such a diverse range of human activities, and in part from the fact that any of these activities can be examined from a variety of perspectives.

When writing is considered by a number of specialists, each of them having the priorities of a different academic discipline or form of writing in mind, there can be no guarantee that what emerges will be a coherent picture of the phenomenon that all claim to be concerned with. On the contrary, the attempt to reconcile assumptions and findings from different fields may well produce confusion rather than enlightenment. Seen from these different perspectives, writing seems to dissolve or disperse into a number of disparate processes or activities which lack any intuitively felt unity. There is no simple answer that can be given today to the question 'What is writing?', and perhaps there never was.

It is nevertheless tempting to think at first that one can grasp – and perhaps even solve – the problem by considering what there is in common between all the possible messages that could be put into written form, or between the various possible ways of putting any one such message into written form. But further reflection suggests that this strategy would be naive for at least three reasons. In the first place, to decide what counts as 'written form' involves answering the question originally asked. In other words, the method proposed is circular. In the second place, it begs the question of whether 'messages' exist at some abstract level before being formulated in writing, and whether they can indeed be 'the same' message if formulated differently. Third, even if pursuit of this strategy were to produce an impressive inventory of alternative possibilities for putting messages into written form, looking for common factors would no more answer the question 'What is writing?' than identifying the common items on a list of possible breakfast menus (with-or-without corn flakes, coffee, grapefruit juice, etc.) would provide an adequate definition of the concept 'breakfast'.

To suppose, in short, that the question 'What is writing?' can be answered by careful examination of many different samples of writing given in advance is symptomatic of a failure to understand the basic conceptual problem.

Throughout the Western tradition, discussions of this problem have been marked by two tendencies. Both are potential sources of misunderstanding and oversimplification. One is the tendency to identify writing with its physical execution, its material resources and processes. The other is the tendency to identify writing with its various social or intellectual functions (whatever these are assumed to be). Different disciplines vary in their liability to succumb to one of these tendencies or the other.

Philosophers, for instance, seem prone to the second. Aristotle is a conspicuous example of a philosopher who evidently believed that once the basic function of writing had been identified, there was little more of interest to be said about the activity in general. Unfortunately, Aristotle's definition of writing applies only to what might more accurately be called 'glottic writing': that is, to forms of writing related specifically to spoken language. A more revealing example is to be found in the eighteenth century in the *Encyclopédie* of Diderot and d'Alembert. Its particular relevance in the present context derives from the fact that the editors of the *Encyclopédie* were much exercised by the problem of drawing up a comprehensive schema of knowledge, of which the structure would reflect the natural divisions between different branches of study. It is thus of great interest to see exactly how and where they fit writing into the totality of human concerns; all the more so since the very feasibility of the *Encyclopédie* project itself depended essentially upon writing in one of its many forms (i.e. the printed book).

The answer is supplied unequivocally in the *Prospectus* to the great work.[2] There the reader is told that the *science de l'homme* is ordered according to the faculties of man, of which the main ones are the understanding and the will. The former has truth as its object and the latter virtue. Hence a primary division between logic on the one hand and morality on the other. Logic in turn subdivides into the art of thinking, the art of retaining one's thoughts and the art of communicating them. The second of these subdivisions has two branches: the science of memory and the science of memory's substitutes. The latter fall under the general category of 'artificial representations', of which writing is one.

This Enlightenment approach has a broader basis than Aristotle's and does not presuppose that writing exists only to record speech. The salient point to note for present purposes is that – contrary perhaps to all modern expectations – writing is *not* here counted as one of the ways available for transmitting thoughts. Nor in the formation of thoughts is writing accorded any role whatever. Its sole function is to *retain* the products of thought and to preserve them by artificial means.

Clearly, this distribution of functions excludes, among other things, the possibility of treating writing as an independent mode of communication (a possibility which will emerge as crucial in the present study). Furthermore, if the *Encyclopédie* classification is taken at face value, writing has a curiously restricted capacity even as a mnemonic device. For all it records

---

2   Jean le Rond d'Alembert, *Discours préliminaire de l'Encyclopédie* (Paris: Gonthier, 1965), pp. 121–68.

is a thought or series of thoughts already formed in accordance with the laws of logic.

The factors lying behind this very specific identification of the function of writing are complex and fall outside the scope of the present discussion. But one aspect is worth comment in passing. The claim that writing has a strictly mnemonic function subtly underwrites both the *Encyclopédie* itself as an enterprise masterminded by philosophers and, at the same time, the role of logic as the key to knowledge. It is a claim that blocks off any philosophical difficulties of the kind that might arise if writing were considered as the actual mode of *transmission* of knowledge or, even more radically, as a possible source of *production* of knowledge. In other words, the demotion of writing to a mere set of mnemonic devices renders it inert and completely unproblematic from a philosophical point of view (or at least no more problematic than tying a knot in a handkerchief to remind you of something that might otherwise be forgotten). To see this is to see that, disinterested though philosophy may claim to be, the philosopher is not always a completely impartial witness to the status of writing.

Historians of writing, on the other hand, are prone to the complementary academic prejudice which treats writing as a set of scripts (hieroglyphic, alphabetic, etc.) and techniques (clay tablets, pen and ink, printing, etc.) to be studied – as it is sometimes put – 'in and for themselves'. This perspective inevitably highlights the material aspects of writing and its material products, with only minimal reference to the function or functions that these systems and techniques are assumed to subserve. Furthermore, histories of writing tend to adopt a narrow view of their subject, neglecting non-glottic forms of writing such as mathematical and musical texts, which can be treated from a historical point of view as secondary or derivative. This neglect amounts in effect to defining writing as a representation of speech, as distinct from a mnemonic for thought.

Psychologists on the whole share this view, although for a different reason. The psychological perspective is one which treats the written text either as the product of skills acquired by the writer or as a point of departure for the exercise of different skills by the reader. In both cases, the focus of attention is upon the acquisition of these skills and the disabilities to which they are subject – a viewpoint which in practice relates closely to the pedagogic concerns of the teacher in the classroom. These concerns have given rise, particularly in recent years, to prolonged and often acrimonious debates over the best way to teach children how to write and read (debates which nevertheless can be traced back as far as Graeco-Roman antiquity). In this perspective, being able to write is to all intents and purposes equated with being able to write one's native language in accordance with the current conventions imposed by predominant educational institutions in one's own culture.

For students of literature and music, however, the material manifestations of writing are of only marginal importance. Writing for them is the process of *composition*, rather than the setting out of the results in a legible form. A 'writer' is a creative artist, whose function is not to be confused with that of the mere amanuensis, secretary or printer, and the literary critic is rarely concerned with the actual manuscript or book, any more than the music critic is interested in the score, except as a document recording 'the work' to be studied. But the work itself is not the written document.

Anthropologists, for their part, have mainly concentrated on the *consequences* of writing – social, political and intellectual. The distinction between societies which have acquired writing and societies which function on the basis of oral communication has been treated as important for a long time – at least since the inclusion of the chapter on 'Writing' in Edward Burnett Tylor's *Anthropology*, where the invention of writing was proclaimed as 'the great movement by which mankind rose from barbarism to civilization'.[3] A later generation of anthropologists disowned this view as ethnocentric, while nevertheless continuing to see writing as a phenomenon of the greatest cultural significance. One anthropologist conspicuously committed to this claim holds that

> there are two main functions of writing. One is the storage function, that permits communication over time and space, and provides man with a marking, mnemonic and recording device. Clearly this function could also be carried out by other means of storage such as the tape-recording of messages. However, the use of aural reproduction would not permit the second function of writing, which shifts language from the aural to the visual domain, and makes possible a different kind of inspection, the re-ordering and refining not only of sentences, but of individual words.[4]

This identification of the functions of writing enables him to propose that literate societies have at their disposal not merely repositories of information from the past but contemporary cognitive tools and modes of knowledge unavailable in a preliterate community.

It is interesting to note that in the passage quoted above, despite its twentieth-century vocabulary, the first part is little more than a restatement of the thesis we have already met in the *Encyclopédie*, where writing was treated as a set of mnemonic devices. It is the second main function of writing which, for this anthropologist, is more important; that is, the replacement of aural storage (such as a tape-recorder provides) by visual storage. But this additional function is no less controversial than the first, for nowhere does the writer offer any demonstration that this comparison is in fact valid, i.e. that writing merely 'shifts' language from one sensory

---

3   E.B. Tylor, *Anthropology* (London: Macmillan, 1881), Ch. VII.
4   J. Goody, *The Domestication of the Savage Mind* (Cambridge: Cambridge University Press, 1977), p. 78.

domain to another. To validate this assumption would require the kind of analysis which anthropology as such has never acknowledged any undertaking to provide – a semiological analysis of the relations between spoken and written texts. It is the same problem that flaws much of the ongoing debate over orality and literacy, a debate which has been in full swing since the influential work of McLuhan in the 1960s.[5]

The above rough sketch of disciplinary perspectives on writing, imperfect though it is, suffices to point to a serious lacuna in the study of writing. Between them, the philosopher, the historian of writing, the educational psychologist, the literary critic and the anthropologist do not provide a very convincing collective answer to the question 'What is writing?' Their divergent approaches are too obviously dictated by the particular interests of their respective disciplines. The same may be said of two other specialists – the philologist and the linguist – who share a concern with certain forms of writing. This diversity of academic perspectives, although interesting in itself, supplies no basis on which to develop any general theory of writing.

Given this situation, it is tempting to cut the Gordian knot by adopting at the outset some stipulative definition of the term *writing* and proceeding on that basis. This is in fact the strategy adopted by many theorists. But far from offering any solution to the conceptual problem referred to above, what this does is make matters worse by misrepresenting the problem itself. To see why, it suffices to examine one such case.

In his paper entitled 'Writing and writing systems', George L. Trager finds no great difficulty in distinguishing writing from other forms of communication that might make use of the same instruments and materials. He invites his reader to consider the differences between three figures (Figs 1.1, 1.2, 1.3). Figure 1.1 is a drawing of an Australian aboriginal shield. Figure 1.2 is part of a street map. Figure 1.3 is part of an anthropologist's chart of a kinship system.

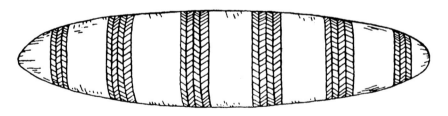

Figure 1.1

---

5   Cf. J. Miller, *McLuhan* (London: Fontana/Collins, 1971). Contributions to the debate include W.J. Ong, *Orality and Literacy* (London: Methuen, 1982) and, more recently, D.R. Olson and N. Torrance (eds), *Literacy and Orality* (Cambridge: Cambridge University Press, 1991).

Figure 1.2

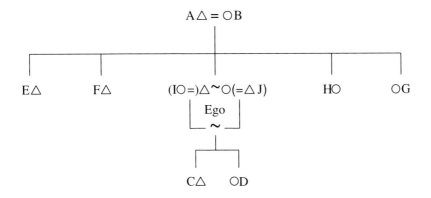

Figure 1.3

Trager imagines his reader's reactions when presented with Figure 1.1 and invited to identify it:

> He can say, 'This is a drawing of some kind of object; it looks like a long ellipse, and is not quite regular. The shadings along the edges suggest that this is perhaps a drawing of something that is a solid body, an elongated ovoid. Or possibly it's just a partly ovoid shell, hollow on the other side. The bands around it may be something made of another material – leather or cloth; but they could be painted. I wonder what it is.'

No two readers, claims Trager, would say exactly the same thing, and even anthropologists who recognized the artifact would not describe it in the same words. This, for Trager, seems to be conclusive proof: 'It is a PICTURE, not a piece of writing.'[6]

Figure 1.2, Trager supposes, would be 'for an American at least, easier to describe and identify'. This American would recognize a configuration of city streets, including at least one 'principal thoroughfare, and some other seemingly dead-end residential streets'. There is also a 'conventional indication of a bridge' and 'so-called clover-leaf access roads'.

> This kind of drawing is 'read' by many people in almost the same terms, if they have learned the conventions of highway maps in the United States. But there is no exact identity of the descriptions; and those who have not learned what a highway map is like may not understand the drawing at all.[7]

It is not until reaching Figure 1.3 that Trager's hypothetical reader begins to find evidence of writing. A student of anthropology will recognize that the triangles indicate males, the circles females, the equation sign marriage, and the single lines descent and consanguineal relationship. But what Trager calls the 'letter labels' are different.

> There are terms for 'father' (A), 'mother' (B), 'son' (C), 'daughter' (D), 'older brother' (E), 'younger brother' (F), 'older sister' (G), 'younger sister' (H), 'wife' (I), 'husband' (J). The double bond, =, and the single lines are, to begin with, signs of relationship; they can be made into writing symbols if the convention is established that = is to be read 'married to', a vertical line is 'descended from' and a horizontal line is 'consanguineally related to'; the symbol ~ is a piece of writing if it is agreed that it is to be read 'or'. If, however, =, |, –, ~ can be read in various

---

6 G.L. Trager, 'Writing and writing systems', p. 378. In T.A. Sebeok (ed.), *Current Trends in Linguistics*, vol. 12 (The Hague/Paris: Mouton, 1974), pp. 373–496.
7 *Ibid.*, p. 378.

equivalent ways. . . then they are signs and not writing symbols. The letter labels are real writing, but they are secondary written symbols, referring to the written form of the words designating the various relationships. When the labels are found in a list, and the terms are noted, then writing is being read.[8]

One of the oddities of Trager's account is that we are not told whether the aborigines have a specific word for the type of shield represented in Figure 1.1. If so, then by Trager's own criteria the configuration shown in Figure 1.1 can function as a written symbol, and his hypothetical American reader's lack of acquaintance with either the word or the object is an irrelevance. Similarly, in the case of Figure 1.2 it is difficult to see what stands in the way of supposing that there might be a cartographer's list of symbols appended to the road map, giving specific verbal equivalents ('bridge', 'dual carriageway', etc.); in which case, again, on Trager's interpretation these configurations become written symbols. But these quibbles are not the main objection to Trager's way of proceeding.

What Trager has done is propose his own definition of the term *writing system* ('conventional system of marks or drawing or analogous artifacts which represents the utterances of a language as such') and then he has applied it to the analysis of three examples. The trouble with this is that the application itself is an exercise in question-begging. Trager's assumption seems to be that what makes a set of marks a writing system is simply an agreement to 'read' the marks by treating them as standing in a fixed correspondence with some specific set of linguistic units; in which case there is nothing – apart from lack of incentive or imagination – to prevent any set of marks from being 'read'.[9]

But worse still, once the issue is treated as one which can be dealt with simply by opting for a preferred definition, it is demoted from a conceptual to a merely terminological problem.[10] In this way, the question of why, for example, 'representing the utterances of a language as such' should be

---

8   *Ibid.*, p. 380.
9   One bizarre consequence of this view would be that what makes it possible to 'read' a musical score is the availability of names for the symbols ('F sharp', 'crescendo', etc.).
10 E.g. for G. Sampson in *Writing Systems* (London: Hutchinson, 1985, p. 30) whether semasiographic symbols count as writing is 'a personal choice about how to use words' (i.e. including the word *writing*). Since Sampson's account of writing pays no further attention to semasiographic systems, the reader is left to infer that this represents Sampson's own personal choice. By this manoeuvre, any contentious theoretical issue whatsoever can be dismissed as merely terminological. Similarly J. Marcus, contrasting the incompatible definitions of writing proposed by Gelb and Diringer, writes 'I prefer the definition of Diringer', as if this were a matter in which anyone could resolve the problem simply by stating a personal preference (J. Marcus, *Mesoamerican Writing Systems* (Princeton, N.J.: Princeton University Press, 1992), p. 17).

treated as *the* function, rather than simply *a* function, of the written sign is ignored altogether.[11]

Similar objections hold against the adoption of any stipulative definition of writing which arbitrarily narrows the field from the outset. Not only does such a move automatically block off certain avenues of enquiry that might have been productive, but at the same time, by conferring a privileged status on certain criteria selected in advance, it inevitably leads to a distorted view of the whole range of graphic signs. In short, proceeding on the basis of a stipulative definition of the term *writing* does nothing to advance anyone's understanding of the subject, and simply creates a theoretical lacuna.

This is the lacuna which semiology should be in a position to fill, for the point of departure for the semiologist is an assumption which all the disciplines mentioned above also make: namely, that writing requires the creation and use of certain kinds of sign. The difference is that whereas the practitioners of other disciplines merely take the existence of the written sign for granted and then focus upon such aspects or such examples of it as suit their own convenience, the business of the semiologist is to probe the theoretical implications of that existence itself and to situate it in relation to the existence of other types of sign. Thus the question 'What is writing?' is tackled from a broader perspective than any imposed by the more specialized disciplines. The written sign becomes not a datum but an explicandum, and its explication becomes accountable to semiological theory.

---

11 In the worst instances, disciplinary blinkers obscure the boundary between facts and definitions altogether. E.g. D. Bolinger claims that 'most writing is the graphic representation of vocal–auditory processes' ('Visual morphemes', *Language*, 22 (1946), p. 333). This is blandly presented as some kind of empirical truth, but is actually a stipulative definition in disguise.

Chapter 2

Integrational semiology

The theory which will here be used as a basis for the analysis of writing is that of integrational semiology.

It is both convenient and historically apposite to take Saussurean semiology as an initial point of reference for explaining the salient features of the integrational approach. The major differences which have implications for a theory of writing may be summarized as follows, pending further amplification in subsequent chapters.

1 Saussure's theory of human communication is telementational. It envisages two individuals (*A* and *B*) attempting to resolve the problem of transferring a thought already formulated independently in one mind (that of *A*) to the other mind (that of *B*). Communication is achieved if and only if the transference is successfully effected, i.e. if the thought *B*'s mind receives is indeed the thought *A*'s mind formulated.[1]

By contrast, the integrational approach views human communication as consisting in the contextualized integration of human activities by means of signs. This approach does not need to restrict communication to a transaction between individuals (*A* and *B*). Nor does it need to define communication by reference to 'thoughts' – however these in turn are defined. (*A fortiori*, it does not need to invoke for definitional purposes the intentions of the participants.) Nor, thirdly, does it need to specify the criteria for successful communication in terms of the *identity* of what is transmitted and what is received.

2 Integration, as the integrationist understands it, involves the non-random linking of sequences of activities. Saussurean semiology shares this perspective up to a point, but imposes limitations upon it. For Saussure, it is not a haphazard connexion which, in the 'speech circuit', links the thought

---

1 For a full discussion of Saussure's theory of communication, see R. Harris, *Reading Saussure* (London: Duckworth, 1987), pp. 204–18. Saussure offers no account of 'partial' or 'incomplete' communication.

which *A* originally formulated, the oral articulation of sounds by *A*, the transmission of sound waves to *B*'s ear, and the triggering of a corresponding thought in *B*'s brain. All this is one highly integrated process, in the sense that each phase depends on the preceding phases. To such an account the integrationist has no objection. But Saussure begs questions which the integrationist would wish to open up. In particular, the integrationist would wish to question (i) Saussure's identification of the initial and terminal points in the chain, and (ii) Saussure's exclusion of all other factors than those involved in the transference process itself. The integrationist would regard as potentially relevant not just these but *all* features of the communication situation in which *A* and *B* find themselves (including the time and place where the event occurs, who *A* and *B* are, their prior dealings with each other, etc.).

3 In Saussurean semiology there is no place for a single, isolated sign. The sign does not exist except as part of a co-existing system of signs, and is defined solely by reference to relations within the system as a whole. Thus the context of communication plays no role whatever in defining the Saussurean sign. In integrational semiology, on the other hand, the sign does not exist outside the context which gives rise to it: there is no abstract invariant which remains 'the same' from one context to the next. Nor, *a fortiori*, is there any overarching Saussurean system to guarantee that invariance.

4 In Saussurean semiology the sign is a bipartite unit. It has a single form (*signifiant*) and a single meaning (*signifié*). The integrational sign has no determinate theoretical structure of this kind: it is treated as a complex of which any number of different facets may be identified, depending on the purpose of the analysis.

5 In Saussurean semiology, a distinction is drawn between the sign itself and its use on any particular occasion. Integrational semiology, on the other hand, treats all signs as unique products of particular communication situations: they are neither the abstract invariants of Saussurean semiology, nor particular instantiations of such invariants.

6 Integrational theory recognizes three sets of factors which typically contribute to the making of any sign: (i) *biomechanical* factors, relating to the capacities of the human organism that determine the parameters within which communication can take place; (ii) *macrosocial* factors, relating to cultural practices and institutions established in particular communities; (iii) *circumstantial* factors, relating to the particular context of communication and the activities integrated.

   A sign is integrational in the sense that it typically involves the contextualized application of biomechanical skills within a certain macrosocial framework, thereby contributing to the integration of activities which would otherwise remain unintegrated.

While biomechanical and macrosocial factors may be studied independently by physiologists, sociologists, etc., there can be no study of signs as such without taking particular circumstances into account. This, at least, is the integrationist's position.

Saussurean semiology is non-integrational because, by abstracting from the specific circumstances of communication, it locates the sign at a different theoretical level. By comparison with the integrational sign, the Saussurean sign is already a second-order entity, presupposing consensus at the macrosocial level. (Thus one of the problems for Saussurean semiology is to explain how the individual can innovate – that is, bring into existence a new sign not accepted by the community and not part of any previous system of signs.)

7 For Saussure, the written sign is a *metasign*, i.e. a sign of some other unit which is itself a sign or part of a sign. Specifically, human speech is assumed to provide the elements to which written signs stand as metasigns. (This feature of Saussurean theory has a long history prior to Saussure, and can be traced back in the Western tradition at least as far as Aristotle. In fact, it does not strictly follow from any postulate of Saussurean semiology, but is introduced independently by Saussure as a working hypothesis.) Thus, without speech writing would not exist. Integrational semiology rejects all these assumptions, both on the general ground that there are other activities than speech that are integrationally related to writing and also because, even where speech and writing *are* integrationally related, they are not necessarily integrated in such a way that the written sign functions as a metasign.

* * *

Substituting integrational premises for Saussurean premises still leaves the semiologist with various possible ways of proceeding. In particular, there remains the question of how different forms of communication might be defined and distinguished one from another.

One possibility might be to select purely biomechanical parameters as setting the limits for a particular form of communication. In the case of writing, vision would be the obvious candidate, i.e. an argument could perhaps be made for restricting the class of written signs to visual signs. A restriction of this kind is often tacitly made in discussions of writing and sometimes acknowledged overtly, as in Gelb's definition of writing: *a system of human intercommunication by means of conventional visible marks.*[2] If this

2 I.J. Gelb, *A Study of Writing* (Chicago: University of Chicago Press, 1952; rev. edn 1963), p. 12.

biomechanical restriction were accepted, then there would come the question of distinguishing within the class of visual signs, and in accordance with the theory of communication adopted, those that belonged to writing.

In the present study, it is not proposed to take any sensory modality as a *fundamentum divisionis* of this kind, and the reasons for this will be explained in due course (Ch. 5).

Chapter 3

A theory of writing

The written sign, however broadly or narrowly we define it, is the product of significant activity on the part of human beings. Semiology is by definition concerned with that significance. But the activity involved in writing may be significant in a number of different ways, not all of which – it might be presumed – necessarily fall within the scope of a semiological theory of writing itself. A preliminary task for the semiologist is to distinguish between these various dimensions of significance and to indicate which of them are pertinent to the semiological analysis proposed.

*   *   *

One way of approaching this preliminary task is to consider various kinds of error, ignorance or misunderstanding which may stand in the way of recognizing a written text for what it is.

Writing, whatever particular form it may take, operates on the basis of relations that may be quite obscure to those who cannot write. This point was evident in the seventeenth century to John Wilkins, who recounts the following anecdote in the preface to *Mercury*, his treatise on cryptography:

> There is a pretty Relation to this purpose concerning an Indian Slave, who being sent by his master, with a Basket of Figs and a Letter, did by the way eat up a great part of his Carriage, conveying the remainder unto the Person to whom he was directed, who when he had read the Letter, and not finding the quantity of Figs answerable to what was there spoken of, he accuses the Slave of eating them, telling him what the letter laid against him. But the Indian (notwithstanding this proof) did confidently abjure the Fact, cursing the Paper, as being a false and lying Witness. After this, being sent again with the like Carriage, and a Letter expressing the just number of Figs that were to be delivered, he did again, according to his former Practice, devour a great part of them by the way; but before he medled with any, (to prevent all following Accusations) he first took the Letter, and hid that under a great Stone, assuring himself, that if it did not see him eat the Figs, it could never tell of him; but being now more strongly accused than before, he confesses the Fault, admiring the

Divinity of the Paper, and for the future does promise his best Fidelity in every Imployment.[1]

Wilkins' anecdote may be compared with the instructive example provided by Lévi-Strauss, who describes the following encounter with the Nambikwara.

It was at this point that there occurred an extraordinary incident that I can only explain by going back a little. It is unnecessary to point out that the Nambikwara have no written language, but they do not know how to draw either, apart from making a few dotted lines or zigzags on their gourds. Nevertheless, as I had done among the Caduveo, I handed out sheets of paper and pencils. At first they did nothing with them, then one day I saw that they were all busy drawing wavy, horizontal lines. I wondered what they were trying to do, then it was suddenly borne upon me that they were writing or, to be more accurate, were trying to use their pencils in the same way as I did mine, which was the only way they could conceive of, because I had not yet tried to amuse them with my drawings. The majority did this and no more, but the chief had further ambitions. No doubt he was the only one who had grasped the purpose of writing. So he asked me for a writing-pad, and when we both had one, and were working together, if I asked for information on a given point, he did not supply it verbally but drew wavy lines on his paper and presented them to me, as if I could read his reply. He was half taken in by his own make-believe; each time he completed a line, he examined it anxiously as if expecting the meaning to leap from the page, and the same look of disappointment came over his face. But he never admitted this, and there was a tacit understanding between us to the effect that his unintelligible scribbling had a meaning which I pretended to decipher; his verbal commentary followed almost at once, relieving me of the need to ask for explanations.

As soon as he had got the company together, he took from a basket a piece of paper covered with wavy lines and made a show of reading it, pretending to hesitate as he checked on it the list of objects I was to give in exchange for the presents offered me: so-and-so was to have a chopper in exchange for a bow and arrows, someone else beads in exchange for necklaces. . . . This farce went on for two hours. Was he perhaps hoping to delude himself? More probably he wanted to astonish his companions, to convince them that he was acting as an intermediary agent for the

---

1 J. Wilkins, *Mercury: or the Secret and Swift Messenger*, 2nd edn (London, 1694), pp. 5–7. This passage may well be the ultimate source of similar anecdotes reported by E.B. Tylor, *Anthropology* (London: Macmillan, 1881), Ch. VII and I.J. Gelb, *A Study of Writing* (Chicago: University of Chicago Press, 1952; rev. edn 1963), Ch. IX.

exchange of the goods, that he was in alliance with the white man and shared his secrets.[2]

A third type of case to be set against the two cited above is that of failure to recognize some particular example of writing as writing. An interesting instance in the history of decipherment is that of Thomas Hyde, Regius Professor of Hebrew and Laudian Professor of Arabic at Oxford in the late eighteenth century, who coined the term *cuneiform*. Paradoxically, Hyde refused to accept that the cuneiform inscriptions of Persepolis were examples of writing and argued that they were merely decorative configurations.[3]

From an integrational point of view, all three cases are different. The slave of Wilkins' anecdote did not even realize what the biomechanical para-meters of writing are: hence his grotesquely misconceived stratagem of hiding the letter. This is a mistake the Nambikwara chief would never have made: he grasped roughly what was involved and went through the motions of writing and reading, even though he clearly did not understand how these processes accomplish what they do. In other words, he failed to grasp the macrosocial dimension of writing. Professor Hyde could both read and write; but could neither read nor write Persian cuneiform (in common with all his contemporaries). He thus failed to appreciate the integrational functions of a particular set of marks.

What the slave of Wilkins' tale failed to understand is something semiologically more fundamental than what the Nambikwara chief failed to understand, which is in turn more fundamental than what Professor Hyde failed to understand. The slave did not grasp even in principle how writing works. The Nambikwara chief failed to understand that it normally involves familiarity with some specific set of marks. The Oxford professor understood both these things, but nevertheless failed to recognize a particular set of marks which was unfamiliar. He therefore concluded that they were not writing. (These differences may be compared to the case of playing card games. We must distinguish between: (i) not understanding what a card game is at all, (ii) understanding what kind of thing is involved in playing cards, but not the significance of the marks on the cards, and (iii) failing to recognize some particular card game – such as bridge – as being a card game.)

For the semiologist of writing, this means that there are at least the following fundamental distinctions to be drawn: between a *theory of written communication*, a *theory of the written sign* and a *theory of writing systems*. Questions concerning the semiological differences between one script and another fall under a theory of writing systems. Questions concerning the form and meaning of units of writing fall under a theory of the written sign.

2 C. Lévi-Strauss, *Tristes Tropiques*, trans. J. Weightman and D. Weightman (London: Cape, 1973), p. 296.
3 M. Pope, *The Story of Decipherment* (London: Thames & Hudson, 1975), p. 88.

Questions concerning the general requirements for the production and interpretation of written texts fall under a theory of written communication.

These three types of theory may be considered the nuclear components of a semiological *theory of writing*.

*   *   *

The relationship between these three components may again be illustrated by reference to the work of Saussure.

1 *Saussure's theory of written communication.* Communication is, for Saussure, a process by which individuals convey their thoughts to one another. In the case of speech, this is done by means of what Saussure calls the 'speech circuit'.

> The starting point of the circuit is in the brain of one individual, for instance *A*, where facts of consciousness which we shall call concepts are associated with representations of linguistic signs or sound patterns by means of which they may be expressed. Let us suppose that a given concept triggers in the brain a corresponding sound pattern. This is an entirely *psychological* phenomenon, followed in turn by a *physiological* process: the brain transmits to the organs of phonation an impulse corresponding to the pattern. Then sound waves are sent from *A*'s mouth to *B*'s ear: a purely *physical* process. Next, the circuit continues in *B* in the opposite order: from ear to brain, the physiological transmission of the sound pattern; in the brain, the psychological association of this pattern with the corresponding concept. If *B* speaks in turn, this new act will pursue – from his brain to *A*'s – exactly the same course as the first, passing through the same successive phases, which we may represent as follows:

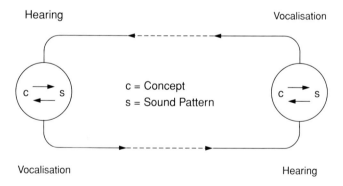

This analysis makes no claim to be complete. One could go on to distinguish the auditory sensation itself, the identification of that sensation with the latent sound pattern, the patterns of muscular movement associated with phonation, and so on. We have included only those elements considered essential; but our schematisation enables us straight away to separate the parts which are physical (sound waves) from those which are physiological (phonation and hearing) and those which are psychological (the sound patterns of words and the concepts). It is particularly important to note that the sound patterns of the words are not to be confused with actual sounds. The word patterns are psychological, just as the concepts associated with them are.[4]

Saussure does not spell out the details of any corresponding account for writing. But from the above passage it is not difficult to reconstruct a Saussurean description of the 'writing circuit', which might run as follows.

The starting point of the circuit is in the brain of one individual, for instance *A*, where representations of linguistic signs are associated with representations of written signs. Let us suppose that a given linguistic sign triggers in the brain a corresponding written sign. This is an entirely *psychological* phenomenon, followed in turn by a *physiological* process: the brain transmits to the hand an impulse corresponding to the written pattern, which the hand transfers on to a surface by means of marks. Then light waves travel from this surface to *B*'s eye: a purely *physical* process. Next, the circuit continues in *B* in the opposite order: from eye to brain, the physiological transmission of the visual pattern; in the brain, the psychological association of this pattern with the corresponding linguistic sign. If *B* writes in turn, this new act will pursue – from his brain to *A*'s – exactly the same course as the first, passing through the same successive phases, which we may represent as follows:

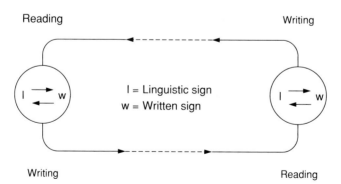

4   F. de Saussure, *Cours de linguistique générale*, 2nd edn (Paris: Payot, 1922), p. 28. All translations are from R. Harris (trans.), *F. de Saussure, Course in General Linguistics* (London: Duckworth, 1983).

This analysis makes no claim to be complete. One could go on to distinguish the visual sensation itself, the identification of that sensation with the latent visual pattern, the patterns of muscular movement associated with writing, and so on. We have included only those elements considered essential; but our schematisation enables us straight away to separate the parts which are physical (light waves) from those which are physiological (inscribing and seeing) and those which are psychological (the visual patterns and the linguistic signs). It is particularly important to note that the visual patterns are not to be confused with actual inscriptions. The visual patterns are psychological, just as the linguistic signs associated with them are.

From an integrational viewpoint, however, there would be something missing from the above account. This lacuna relates to the fact that writing, unlike speech, normally – although not invariably – involves the use of tools.

This feature of the writing process cannot be considered extraneous to it for at least three reasons.

(i)   The use of tools and specially prepared writing surfaces substantially affects the range of activities integrated. A person who has learnt to write using one particular technique cannot automatically transfer those skills to a technique involving different tools. In other words, the use of tools has biomechanical implications.

(ii) Different techniques affect the development of forms of writing and hence may need to be taken into account in a theory of scripts. The use of wax tablets in ancient Rome, baked clay in Babylon, pattra in India, tortoise shell in China, is not unrelated to the form of some of the scripts developed in those regions. Here both biomechanical and macrosocial factors are involved.

(iii) A choice between different techniques of execution may introduce an asymmetry into the Saussurean circuit; that is, *B* may choose a different technique from *A* (but not necessarily a different writing system) in order to reply to *A*'s message. No parallel asymmetry arises in the case of speech. It is not so much the asymmetry *per se* that is important, but the fact that the choice between two techniques of writing may give rise in itself to semiological values. In practice, there seems to be a complex but poorly understood set of interconnexions between the choice of writing technique and the choice of formulation of the written message.

All these considerations point to the need for a *theory of writing techniques* as part of a comprehensive theory of written communication. [5]

5 This topic will not be pursued further in the present study, but remains a promising field for analytic and theoretical exploration. (For further comments, see Ch. 17.)

2 *Saussure's theory of the written sign.* Like the spoken sign, the written sign is, for Saussure, a bipartite unit, comprising the association of a certain form with a certain meaning. The essential differences between spoken signs and written signs reside in (i) the visual nature of the written sign, as opposed to the auditory nature of the spoken sign, and (ii) the fact that the written sign functions only indirectly as a representation of thought (concepts), its immediate function being to represent spoken language. 'A language and its written form constitute two separate systems of signs. The sole reason for the existence of the latter is to represent the former.'[6] Important similarities between the written sign and the spoken sign, according to Saussure, are that both are (i) arbitrary signs and also (ii) linear signs. These are controversial contentions, even within the Saussurean semiological framework, but it is clear that Saussure was committed to them.

3 *Saussure's theory of writing systems.* According to Saussure, there are only two basic types of writing system:

1. The ideographic system, in which a word is represented by some uniquely distinctive sign which has nothing to do with the sounds involved. This sign represents the entire word as a whole, and hence represents indirectly the idea expressed. The classic example of this system is Chinese.
2. The system often called 'phonetic', intended to represent the sequence of sounds as they occur in the word. Some phonetic writing systems are syllabic. Others are alphabetic, that is to say based upon the irreducible elements of speech. [7]

*   *   *

It is evident from the above outline that what Saussure proposes is not a *general* theory of writing, for it does not take non-glottic forms of writing into account at all. Saussure has nothing to say about musical or mathematical notation, for example. But at this point we need not be concerned with the details of Saussure's views. Our immediate interest is simply the theoretical structure of his semiology of writing, taking this as an example of the distinctions set out earlier in the present chapter.

It is clear that there is a rationale linking the theory of communication, the theory of the written sign and the theory of writing systems. This rationale hinges on the acceptance of two very general metatheoretical propositions. One involves a distinction between dependent and independent systems. For Saussure, writing systems, although semiologically *separate*, are not semiologically *independent*: the written sign presupposes the spoken sign, but not vice versa. The second proposition is that a basic distinction

6 Saussure, *Cours*, p. 45.
7 *Ibid.*, p. 47.

is to be drawn between a system and its use. (Terminologically, this distinction is often drawn by Saussure as a distinction between *langue* (system) and *parole* (use); but these terms presuppose speech as the mode of communication in question. No corresponding terms are proposed by Saussure for writing.)

These two propositions, although essential to Saussurean semiology, do not necessarily have to be accepted without question by alternative semiologies of writing. But there is nevertheless a general requirement of explanatory coherence relating the proposed theory of communication to the proposed theory of the written sign and this in turn to the proposed theory of writing systems.

* * *

Finally, a semiological theory of writing may be seen as resting upon certain metaphysical presuppositions.

In Saussure's case, these presuppositions may be described as being broadly those of modern Western empiricism. Integrational semiology – again, broadly – shares these presuppositions. (The caveat implied by the term *broadly* relates mainly to the fact that an integrationist might well accuse Saussure of reifying abstract objects, such as 'languages', and of believing in a Durkheimian 'collective consciousness'.)

But both Saussurean and integrational semiology share, for instance, the assumption that the semiologist has to produce an account which does not rely on some mystical or magical transmission of information. It must be based on sensory perception of physical objects or events.

(Hence the importance in Saussure's theory of the *physical* section of the circuit by which signs are used to convey thoughts. The sign has to have properties that correlate with physically specifiable and physically realizable features. In fact, underlying Saussure's account of the communicational circuit there is also an Aristotelian assumption to which integrational semiology is not committed: see Ch. 6 below.)

In the case of writing, the physical objects produced – written texts – are themselves inanimate: they cannot spontaneously initiate or respond to new communicational demands. The Indian slave of Wilkins' story entertained beliefs about writing which clearly conflict with this metaphysics. Perhaps the Nambikwara chief did too, although this is not clear from the evidence Lévi-Strauss provides. Thomas Hyde, one assumes, did not: whatever his theological convictions, they made no difference to his beliefs about possible forms of writing likely to have been invented and successfully practised by human beings.

Chapter 4

A theory of written communication

A theory of written communication will be an indispensable component of any comprehensive semiological theory of writing. But one theory of written communication may differ from another in its scope: that is to say, in the kind and amount of information assumed to be necessary in order to explain how human beings communicate by writing. This question of scope must now be addressed.

A general distinction may be drawn here between 'restricted' and 'unrestricted' theories. Again, this may be illustrated by reference to Saussure. As has already been pointed out, Saussure is concerned only with glottic writing, not with writing in general. But his approach is also 'restricted' in another sense. The Saussurean theory of written communication sketched in the preceding chapter might be regarded, even for glottic writing, as the very minimum that will qualify as a theoretical account. All it treats as relevant are the following factors: (i) the availability to both *A* and *B* of the same writing system, (ii) the opportunity for *B* to read what *A* has written and vice versa, and (iii) the abilities of both *A* and *B* to formulate, execute and comprehend the written messages correctly in accordance with the writing system chosen. *Mutatis mutandis*, these are exactly the same communicational requirements as in Saussure's theory of speech communication, and the same model could obviously be extended to other types of communication system.

For an integrationist, the question arises whether such a restricted theory can address all the semiologically pertinent factors that inevitably arise when we take into account the varied contexts in which written communication occurs; and the *prima facie* answer to this question must be that it cannot.

For one thing, the act of writing may have significance in itself, *irrespective of what is written down*. Writing and reading, unlike speech, have in many cultures remained accomplishments restricted to a privileged professional class. Evidence of such accomplishments may consequently acquire the status of social and political signs in their own right. This may even happen, as Lévi-Strauss shrewdly observes in the case of his Nambikwara chief, in circumstances where the individual in fact only *appears* to have the accomplishments in question:

> Writing had, on that occasion, made its appearance among the Nambikwara but not, as one might have imagined, as a result of long and laborious training. It had been borrowed as a symbol, and for a sociological rather than an intellectual purpose, while its reality remained unknown. It had not been a question of acquiring knowledge, of remembering or understanding, but rather of increasing the authority and prestige of one individual – or function – at the expense of others. A native still living in the Stone Age had guessed that this great means towards understanding, even if he was unable to understand it, could be made to serve other purposes.[1]

A quite different type of case in which the act of writing may itself acquire significance is memorably captured in George Orwell's novel *Nineteen Eighty-Four*, when Winston Smith decides to begin keeping a diary:

> He went back to the living-room and sat down at a small table that stood to the left of the telescreen. From the table drawer he took out a penholder, a bottle of ink, and a thick, quarto-sized blank book with a red back and a marbled cover.
>
> For some reason the telescreen in the living-room was in an unusual position. Instead of being placed, as was normal, in the end wall, where it could command the whole room, it was in the longer wall, opposite the window. To one side of it there was a shallow alcove in which Winston was now sitting, and which, when the flats were built, had probably been intended to hold bookshelves. By sitting in the alcove, and keeping well back, Winston was able to remain outside the range of the telescreen, so far as sight went. He could be heard, of course, but so long as he stayed in his present position he could not be seen. It was partly the unusual geography of the room that had suggested to him the thing that he was now about to do.
>
> But it had also been suggested by the book that he had just taken out of the drawer. It was a peculiarly beautiful book. Its smooth creamy paper, a little yellowed by age, was of a kind that had not been manufactured for at least forty years past. He could guess, however, that the book was much older than that. He had seen it lying in the window of a frowsy little junk-shop in a slummy quarter of the town (just what quarter he did not now remember) and had been stricken immediately by an overwhelming desire to possess it. Party members were supposed not to go into ordinary shops ('dealing on the free market', it was called), but the rule was not

---

1   C. Lévi-Strauss, *Tristes Tropiques*, trans. J. Weightman and D. Weightman (London: Cape, 1973), pp. 297–8.

strictly kept, because there were various things such as shoelaces and razor blades, which it was impossible to get hold of in any other way. He had given a quick glance up and down the street and then had slipped inside and bought the book for two dollars fifty. At the time he was not conscious of wanting it for any particular purpose. He had carried it guiltily home in his briefcase. Even with nothing written in it, it was a compromising possession.

The thing he was about to do was to open a diary. This was not illegal (nothing was illegal, since there were no longer any laws), but if detected it was reasonably certain that it would be punished by death, or at least by twenty-five years in a forced-labour camp. Winston fitted a nib into the penholder and sucked it to get the grease off. The pen was an archaic instrument, seldom used even for signatures, and he had procured one, furtively and with some difficulty, simply because of a feeling that the beautiful creamy paper deserved to be written on with a real nib instead of being scratched with an ink-pencil. Actually, he was not used to writing by hand. Apart from very short notes, it was usual to dictate everything into the speakwrite which was of course impossible for his present purpose. He dipped the pen into the ink and then faltered for just a second. A tremor had gone through his bowels. To mark the paper was the decisive act. In small clumsy letters he wrote:

April 4th, 1984.[2]

In this passage the phrase 'even with nothing written in it' is particularly noteworthy: that is to say, it is not *what* one writes but the mere acquisition of materials for producing a written text which is politically suspect in the society Orwell describes. Hence the act of writing itself – again, regardless of what is written – becomes in advance a political act, a sign of dissidence.

The political regime under which Winston lives is one which has discovered the truth that to control the past is to control the future. Hence its ceaseless programme of revising all records of the past in accordance with decisions subsequently taken. Literacy is a dangerous accomplishment in such a society, affording the reader independent access to 'uncorrected' historical documents.

Every act of writing is not necessarily a political act: whether it is or not will depend on the context. But what this fictional case illustrates in a particularly dramatic form is something of direct relevance to semiological theory. In the first place, the significance acquired by the act of writing will depend on the role played by writing within the totality of beliefs and practices current in any given society. In the second place, the simple fact that writing – unlike speech – may not be within the grasp of all members

---

2   G. Orwell, *Nineteen Eighty-Four* (London: Secker & Warburg, 1949). Repr. Harmondsworth: Penguin, 1987, pp. 8–9.

of society is a fact which in itself gives rise to a certain social distribution of that ability and thereby institutes a set of values associated with it.

Now it might be argued that, in both the non-fictional case of the Nambikwara as well as the fictional case of Orwell's society, the values in question are symbolic, social, political, etc. and therefore fall outside the proper scope of a theory of writing. But from an integrational point of view, that would be an attempt to draw a line where none can be drawn. To the extent that a political gesture is implemented in an appropriate context by an act of writing, the act in question becomes a sign, and the significance of that sign calls for explication: that is, we are entitled to ask what role *writing* plays in these cases and why.

Such an explication is precisely what is provided on the one hand by Lévi-Strauss's commentary on the Nambikwara 'writing lesson' and on the other by Orwell's detailed account of the circumstances in which Winston Smith writes *April 4th, 1984.*

Particular explications, it need hardly be stressed, may be disputed for one reason or another. But the point is that without knowing the kind of background information that Orwell gives us we should not be in any position to understand just what Winston's act signifies and in what danger he thereby places himself. Certainly, poring over *the text* that Winston produces will fail to enlighten us. How could the written forms *April 4th, 1984* possibly give any clue? We should be equally puzzled if, without knowing the context, we were to inspect the wavy lines on the Nambikwara chief's 'list' of exchanges.

Once we concede the possibility that the act of writing may itself be significant, we can no longer exclude the possibility that this significance (be it motivated by political, social, religious or other circumstances) may, in certain contexts, constrain in various ways what gets to be written down. A theory of writing cannot afford to neglect those constraints. If it did, it would be guilty of decontextualizing the whole writing process.

To put the point in terms of a theory of written communication, the choice is between having a theory in which the human agents are totally anonymous figures (like Saussure's *A* and *B*), the content of the hypothetical written message is unknown and the circumstances of its being written are not divulged, and, on the other hand, an integrational theory in which it is treated as potentially relevant to know who *A* and *B* are, what the written message is and all the circumstantial details. But between these two extremes there is no theoretically justifiable point at which a line can be drawn, i.e. no reason for excluding *in principle* some kinds of information while treating other kinds of information as semiologically pertinent.

What kind of information may be relevant will depend on the context. The case of signing a document provides an obvious instance where the personal identity of the signatory is semiologically pertinent (see Ch. 11).

There will be documents which A can sign whereas B cannot (except under pain of committing a forgery). The signature is a written sign of which the significance is not exhausted by the linguistic information it ostensibly records, viz. A's name. This is not to assume that the practice of signing documents is semiologically institutionalized in all literate societies; but the fact that it is in some societies is sufficient to point up the inadequacy of any theory of written communication which treats the identity of the writer as semiologically irrelevant.

To accept the above arguments means opting for an 'unrestricted' theory of written communication in preference to a 'restricted' theory, on the ground that no class of restrictions can be laid down that is guaranteed in advance *not* to exclude communicationally significant features of the act of writing. An integrational theory of the kind that will be developed in the following chapters is an 'unrestricted' theory in this sense.

Chapter 5

Writing and temporality

Opting for an 'unrestricted' theory of writing throws into sharp relief the need to address the general question of the biomechanical constraints on writing as a form of communication.

For the integrationist the key factor here is not sensory modality but time. Time takes priority because time, being common to all sensory modalities, is the primary axis along which, for human beings, the various senses are themselves integrated. Human time, it might be argued, is essentially an intellectual construction based on that integration of sensory information; but that is a philosophical issue which cannot be pursued here.

For present purposes, all that need be posited is that in every act of human communication there is implicit an integration of past, present and possible future activities. Without this temporal structuring, communication would be an entirely different process. Making sense of messages would demand a logic we can only apprehend imaginatively on the level of science fiction, but neither comprehend nor actually engage in.

No message is timeless. But certain forms of communication, of which writing is one, are distinguished by the way they allow certain time-gaps to be bridged.

There is no great mystery about this, as may be seen by considering the common practice of keeping a diary. The diary tends to be overlooked by theorists who assume that communication is essentially a process linking two or more individuals. Indeed, the notion of a single individual being both sender and receiver of the same message is sometimes regarded as problematic or paradoxical. ('How can I tell myself what I already know?') But whereas talking to oneself is often treated as a sign of mental disturbance, writing to oneself – particularly in the form of memos or diaries – is widely accepted.

The basic rationale of this practice is simple: people do it in order to remind themselves of what they might otherwise forget. (But this in itself does not warrant treating the primary purpose of the written sign as being mnemonic. The error made by the many thinkers, from Plato onwards, who have viewed writing as an essentially mnemonic device is that of mistaking this aspect of the temporality of writing for its communicative function.)

Perhaps the point would be better put this way: if we lived on a planet where the only writing surfaces and writing instruments available were of a kind that rendered a written text no less ephemeral than speech – that is, if the written word disappeared from sight just as quickly as the spoken word ceased to be audible – then there would be no such activity as keeping a diary.

This, although obvious, is worth stressing: for there are indeed modes of visual communication no less ephemeral than speech. (The sign language of the deaf is one example.) And a comparison of these with writing brings into focus another metaphysical premiss: that the written text is an object, not an event. This premiss qualifies as metaphysical because the distinction between objects and events is itself a metaphysical distinction.

The connexion between writing and gesture has been discussed by various authors. Garrick Mallery, for example, describes picture-writing as 'the direct and durable expression of ideas of which gesture language gives the transient expression'.[1]

If we probe the notion of transience in such cases, it seems that the criterion of transience is the failure of any stable object to materialize.

Sky-writing is an interesting marginal case; and its marginality confirms the above analysis. We have the same problem with the 'objecthood' of sky-writing as with the objecthood of clouds. And it is possible to envisage a whole range of intermediate hypothetical cases, exhibiting different degrees and modes of impermanence.

This problem of the temporal status of the written sign is sometimes ignored by theorists who nevertheless feel free to assume in their discussions of writing that written texts are guaranteed some kind of enduring existence. As a result, one notices a tendency to speak as if what mainly distinguishes writing from speech is its sensory modality (visual versus auditory); and yet the characteristics of writing that are singled out as important turn out to relate not to the visual transmission of the message but rather to the enduring trace it leaves behind. Thus, for example, Goody claims that

> Writing makes speech 'objective' by turning it into an object of visual as well as aural inspection; it is the shift of the receptor from ear to eye, of the producer from voice to hand.[2]

But when it comes to explaining exactly why this transformation is important, it emerges that what Goody finds significant is not the visibility of writing but the quasi-permanence of the written form:

1 G. Mallery, *Picture-Writing of the American Indians* (Washington: Government Printing Office, 1893). Repr. New York: Dover, 1972, vol. I, p. 26.
2 J. Goody, *The Domestication of the Savage Mind* (Cambridge: Cambridge University Press, 1977), p. 44.

when an utterance is put in writing it can be inspected in much greater detail, in its parts as well as its whole, backwards as well as forwards, out of context as well as in its setting; in other words, it can be subjected to a quite different type of scrutiny and critique than is possible with purely verbal communication. [3]

Even when we set aside Goody's confusion of verbal communication with oral communication and his question-begging talk of 'inspecting' an utterance, it is apparent that he here conflates the visual with the static. None of his points would be valid if writing, although visual, were as ephemeral as speech (i.e. if the beginning of any written sentence had already disappeared by the time the end came in sight).

Other theorists, however, treat the durability of the written message as a more important feature than its visual modality in explaining how the introduction of writing transformed human life. Gusdorf, for example, claims:

The invention of writing overthrew the first human world and permitted the development of a new mental age. It is no exaggeration to say that it constitutes one of the essential features in the disappearance of the mythical world of prehistory. Speech had given to man domination of his immediate space. But, bound to the concrete present, it can attain in scope and duration only an horizon limited to the fleeting boundaries of consciousness. Writing permits the separation of the voice from the present reality and thereby expands its range. Writings remain, and by that means they have the power to fix the world, to stabilize it in duration. Likewise they crystallize and give form to a personality which then becomes capable of signing his name and of making himself felt beyond his bodily limits. Writing consolidates speech. It creates a deposit which can wait indefinitely for its reactivation in some consciousness to come. The historic personality poses before future generations. He inscribes on basalt, granite, or marble the chronicle of his deeds.[4]

If there is no requirement that a written text be an object, rather than an event, then in principle there is no reason why communication by gesture should not count as writing. To concede this, however, would put the whole history of writing into a new and unfamiliar perspective: writing might then precede speech in human evolution.[5]

Some theorists, doubtless sensing this difficulty, have incorporated the

3 *Ibid.*, p. 44.
4 G. Gusdorf, *Speaking*, trans. P.T. Brockelman (Evanston: Northwestern University Press, 1965), p. 111.
5 This has in fact been argued by J. van Ginneken in 'Die Bilderschrift-Sprachen', *Travaux du Cercle Linguistique de Prague*, 8 (1939) and 'La reconstruction typologique des langues archaïques de l'humanité', *Verhandelingen der K. Nederlandsche Akademie van Wetenschappen* (Letterkunde, NR xliv), Amsterdam, 1940.

requirement of durability into their definitions of writing; but apparently without taking into account the fact that modern recording techniques have given the spoken word a potential durability which rivals that of writing. Thus Josef Vachek defines written language (as distinct from spoken language) as 'a system of signs which can be manifested graphically and whose function is to respond to a given stimulus (which, as a rule, is not urgent) in a static way, i.e., the response should be permanent (i.e., preservable)'.[6] The hesitation betrayed in the gloss 'permanent (i.e., preservable)' is revealing, the two terms not being synonymous. Evidently the problem is that permanence is too strong a requirement and preservability too weak if the theorist is looking for a criterion that will differentiate writing from speech.

This is patently a crucial issue for the theory of written communication. To leave it in metaphysical limbo is clearly unsatisfactory. By creating objects that can preserve ephemeral events of the past in very considerable auditory and visual detail, modern technology might seem to have blurred a formerly clear distinction which placed writing in a quite separate category of communication both from speech and from gesture. At the very least, it forces theorists of writing to scrutinize their criteria far more carefully. What this scrutiny reveals is that a vague appeal to durability will no longer do.

The fact is that once again, as in the past, the introduction of new technologies has extended the boundaries of writing. What lags behind is our conceptualization of the change. This is what produces the modern 'problem' of defining writing. We seem to be faced with a choice between clinging to old definitions which no longer correspond to new technological possibilities or adjusting to more radical definitions which somehow lose touch with what we had always assumed writing to be. In a technological world where speech can be recalled from the past at the touch of a button, and face-to-face interactions can be summoned up from storage and displayed temporarily on a screen just as easily as passages of text, are the traditional distinctions between various modes of communication finally breaking down?

It is not immediately obvious how Saussurean semiology can solve the problem posed by the durability of writing. Integrational semiology, on the other hand, is in a position to propose a clear and well-motivated solution.

For when communication is considered from an integrational point of view it becomes clear that various issues run the risk of being confused here. In the integrated sequences linking the formation, processing and interpretation of signs (see Ch. 9), temporality becomes semiologically relevant in at least two different ways. There is the question of whether the sign (as

6   J. Vachek, 'Written language and printed language', *Recueil Linguistique de Bratislava*, I (1948), pp. 67–75. Repr. in J. Vachek (ed.), *A Prague School Reader in Linguistics* (Bloomington: Indiana University Press, 1964), pp. 453–60.

distinct from its *formation*) has itself a kinetic dimension. If so, this will have certain processing implications, since all movement is temporally articulated. But there is also the quite separate question – arising from the fact that processing in any case takes time – of the minimum duration required for effective processing to take place.

Communication inevitably breaks down whenever that minimum cannot be met, for whatever reason. And the issue is not whether we should or should not apply the term *writing* to visual or other forms presented so fleetingly as to be unprocessable: the point, rather, is that if writing were invariably like that it would not be a viable form of communication at all. So here at least we have one biomechanical time-related parameter which it is difficult to ignore. Communication needs to be *slow* enough to work. (A lesson it is difficult to learn in an age when faster communication is automatically equated with better communication.)

It is the kinetic criterion, however, that distinguishes written communication from gestural communication, as it likewise distinguishes any static art form (e.g. painting[7]) from any kinetic art form (e.g. ballet).[8] The written form as such has no kinetic dimension, even though its formation may require precisely trained movements of the pen, brush, stylus, etc.; whereas the gestural form is intrinsically kinetic. If *A* and *B* communicate by gestures, then each must watch what the other *does*, that is, the actual movements of formation. The difference, from an integrational viewpoint, hinges on the logic of the temporal relationship between formation and processing in the two types of case.[9]

Here again, there is no question of attempting to legislate for the term *writing*, or even of finding a plausible justification for its lay usage. Whatever we call the forms separated by the kinetic criterion, the fact remains that they fall into semiologically different categories.

It is not simply that the difference between kinetic and non-kinetic forms, together with the processing implications of that difference, are deeply rooted in human physiology. What is crucial is that to this difference there corresponds an important macrosocial division between modes of interaction. That convergence brings us to a level which is

---

7 So-called 'action painting' provides confirmation, not disproof, of this. Rosenberg's famous dictum that the canvas is 'an arena in which to act' means inevitably that the resultant painting is seen as a direct record of the artist's actions, which in some sense have to be reconstructed by the viewer from that record.

8 The difference between mobile sculpture and static sculpture offers a direct comparison. Mobile sculpture exploits configurational possibilities that static sculpture can do no more than hint at, even when both use exactly the same three-dimensional shapes. Calder's mobiles are not just insecure static sculptures that the maker has omitted to fix properly.

9 In one case, but not the other, *B* has to monitor *A*'s activity of formation in order to engage in processing and interpretation (see Ch. 9). This is precisely the difference between semaphore and gesture. But it would of course be perfectly possible from an integrational point of view to 'develop' semaphore into a genuine kinetic form of communication (i.e. by dispensing with the alphabetic interpretation of the static flag positions).

presumably the most fundamental for any theoretical enterprise in this area; or at least it is difficult to see what more fundamental level a theorist could appeal to in the field of human communication. That is, we are talking about basic biomechanical facts that affect human relations all the way from the interpersonal to the international scale.

For when the form of the sign has a kinetic dimension, it cannot be reprocessed (i.e. any further processing by a human being requires replication of the original form, with all the problems that entails). But any non-kinetic form can, in principle, be processed and reprocessed as often as may be, and by as many people as have access to it, within the temporal limits determined by its own duration. That duration will be subject to the uncertainties that apply to all physical objects. The fact that some written texts, like some paintings, may last for hundreds of years, while others are destroyed almost as soon as they are completed, does not affect the issue. To that extent, the durability question – as usually posed in connexion with writing – is badly posed. Something that is temporally contingent is confused with something that is not.

Once the Rubicon of reprocessing is crossed, we enter a world in which communication between human beings is on a different footing altogether, the world of ephemeral messages. Speech belongs to this world. Why is it a different world? Because we are not physiologically equipped to reprocess a spoken message auditorily unless the acoustic signal is replicated. *Mutatis mutandis*, the same applies to gesture.[10] This is communication in which there are no second chances, no physiological possibility of checking or re-examining the message. It is communication in which, without access to a repetition of the signal, all subsequent assessment is memory-dependent. As such, it belongs to a different order of human interactions from communication which is not restricted in this way. Life is not the same under these two conditions.

Anyone who doubts whether there is a fundamental difference here would do well to reflect on, for instance, the impact which technologies such as photography and sound recording have had on standards of evidence in courts of law. We no longer rely on the fallible memory of witnesses when a videotape of the incident is available.

Writing is a technology of the same order: it produces evidence which is not memory-dependent. And the reason for this, the possibility of rereading what is written, is also what makes it possible to keep a diary. Thus the diary is not just an adventitious by-product of writing, but a highly significant application of it.

10   It is, obviously, possible in certain circumstances to control communication in such a way that non-kinetic visual forms are in effect rendered non-reprocessable, as for instance in flashing a message momentarily on a screen. But this is a different case from the inherent non-reprocessability of gesture.

It should be noted nevertheless that according to the view proposed here writing is a form of communication with at least one reasonably clear biomechanical limitation. It is this limitation which, for instance, precludes the possibility of developing auditory forms of writing – and not an arbitrary decision by the theorist to erect the lay use of the terms *spoken* and *written* into a categorial distinction.

Furthermore, the implications of the integrationist's reprocessing criterion are more far-reaching than might initially appear. A semiology based on this criterion is in a position to explain something which Saussurean semiology cannot: the interdependence of our concepts of communication and self. Our willingness to assimilate the case of *A* delivering a message to *B*, here and now, to the case of an earlier *A* sending a message to a later *A*, who *ex hypothesi* is not present here and now, is no small matter, either psychologically or philosophically. What makes the notion of 'communication with oneself' viable in the case of writing but problematic in the case of speech (before the advent of sound recording) is the common temporal scheme into which we fit both our understanding of the activity of communication and our understanding of the continuity of the self.

The advent of writing was in that respect a far more momentous innovation for humanity than any innovation in communication that occurred before or has occurred since. Integrating knowledge of an earlier self with knowledge of a later self became a semiological process subject to conscious control and evaluation.

Chapter 6

Writing and space

Valentin Haüy (1745–1822), founder of the Institution Nationale des Jeunes Aveugles in Paris, is credited with the discovery that the blind are able to read alphabetic script by touch if the letters are embossed.[1] It was his pupil Louis Braille (1809–52) who devised the six-dot matrix of marks which became the system still known as braille writing.

This development is commonly treated by historians of writing as a late, fortuitous and minor episode in the evolution of the alphabet. In fact, it raises an issue of fundamental theoretical importance concerning writing in general.

What Haüy stumbled upon was a truth that had eluded countless generations of sighted writers and readers; namely, that the underlying formal substratum of writing is not visual but spatial.

This discovery provides the second biomechanical basis for an integrational theory of writing, and points to an analysis of written syntagmatics in terms of the organization of graphic space (Ch. 18).

* * *

How is this organization related to the temporality of writing (Ch. 5)? The connexion turns on the biomechanical fact that the formation, processing and interpretation of written forms (Ch. 9) all take time. Thus the way graphic space is organized is not ultimately independent of these temporal activities. What an individual can do 'at once' is very limited. Beyond those limits, we move sequentially. So even if we can 'take in' a page at a glance, we can seldom read what is written on it at a glance, unless there is very little written on it and its spatial organization is not too complex.

Modern reading experiments show – not surprisingly – that the traditional horizontal 'line' of alphabetic writing is by no means the optimum organizational unit of graphic space as far as visual processing is concerned. In all established writing traditions, and arguably in any written text

---

1 However, the idea of using tangible letters for the blind to read is older and goes back at least to the sixteenth century.

whatsoever, the spatial arrangement of written forms represents a compromise of some kind between the requirements of the writer and those of the reader. What is of interest to the semiologist is not so much how these compromises are reached – which in many cases it may be impossible to determine – but rather how, when reached, they provide for the use of space to articulate signification.

*   *   *

It is the availability of space for the deployment of written forms which gives the syntagmatics of writing far greater variety and complexity than the syntagmatics of speech could ever have. In the case of speech, the biomechanics of the vocal apparatus confine the structure of utterance to the modification of a single, continuous stream of sound, which can be interrupted and varied in volume and quality, but cannot use two- or three-dimensional contrasts of any kind.

This limitation on speech means that every traditional form of glottic writing inevitably misrepresents the nature of the speech signal, although this misrepresentation is both masked and compounded by those theorists who describe the spoken sign as being 'linear'.[2] The term is a misnomer. The properties of a line are not those of speech. Furthermore, the term 'linear' highlights precisely those characteristics of the written form which it derives from the use of spatial relations and thus distinguish it from speech and all other forms of auditory communication.

There simply is no counterpart in speech to the use of a surface, which is the commonest way in writing of articulating spatial relations (Ch. 17).

Nor is there any counterpart in speech to the way in which it is possible in writing to vary the disposition of marks on a surface in accordance with the changing spatial relations between the reader and that surface (Plate 8). Here we see a further aspect of the way in which spatial and temporal relations intermesh in writing: because the reader is assumed to be moving, and thus reaching one potential processing point before another, the spatial relations between forms on the writing surface are adjusted accordingly.

*   *   *

From the biomechanical parameters so far identified, writing emerges as a form of communication which integrates past, present and future activities by means of the organization of non-kinetic configurations in space.

However, this also appears to be true in general of certain other forms of communication (e.g. drawing and related graphic arts) which show similar temporal and spatial characteristics. Is writing to be distinguished from these? If so, how? If not, are all such forms in some sense writing?

It is tempting to try to press into service for this purpose Peirce's well-

2   E.g. F. de Saussure: see *Cours de linguistique générale*, 2nd edn (Paris: Payot, 1922), p. 103.

known distinction between iconic and symbolic signs. An icon is described by Peirce as

> a sign which refers to the Object that it denotes merely by virtue of characters of its own, and which it possesses, just the same, whether any such Object actually exists or not. It is true that unless there really is such an Object, the Icon does not act as a sign; but this has nothing to do with its character as a sign. Anything whatever, be it quality, existent individual, or law, is an Icon of anything, in so far as it is like that thing and used as a sign of it.[3]

A symbol, on the other hand, is

> a sign which refers to the Object that it denotes by virtue of a law, usually an association of general ideas, which operates to cause the Symbol to be interpreted as referring to that Object.[4]

Thus the spatial configuration of lines in the drawing of a tree would be iconic of the spatial configuration of features of the tree itself, whereas the configuration of lines in the written word *tree* would not be.

But to distinguish in general between drawing and writing along these lines is not a viable option. For one thing, the distinction as defined by Peirce is drawn in such a way that certain algebraic formulae turn out to be iconic and thus fall into the same category as pictures.

> When, in algebra, we write equations under one another in a regular array, especially when we put resembling letters for corresponding coefficients, the array is an icon. Here is an example:

$$a_1x + b_1y = n_1,$$
$$a_2x + b_2y = n_2.$$

> This is an icon, in that it makes quantities look alike which are in analogous relations to the problem. In fact, every algebraical equation is an icon, in so far as it *exhibits*, by means of the algebraical signs (which are not themselves icons), the relations of the quantities concerned.[5]

Now if this is the case for algebraic formulae, it presumably applies equally to similar cases in glottic writing. Thus, for instance, if the spellings *minimum* and *minimal* are regarded as denoting the pronunciation of those words, they are iconic forms in so far as the letters exhibit a similarity between them that answers to a phonetic similarity. So the distinction between writing and drawing cannot be based on Peirce's distinction between symbol and icon.

In any case, Peirce's theory of signs is surrogational (Ch. 7) and thus falls outside the semiological framework adopted here.

3   J. Buchler (ed.), *Philosophical Writings of Peirce* (New York: Dover, 1955), p. 102.
4   *Ibid.*, p. 102.
5   *Ibid.*, p. 107.

For the integrational semiologist, any such distinction(s) must be drawn not at the level of the individual graphic units but in terms of the way the units are deployed in graphic space. The immediately preceding sentence, for example, uses a syntagmatic device – the parenthetic *(s)* – and this sentence uses another – italicization – which correspond to no customary features of pictorial practice in the Western tradition. There are typical differences of this kind between the ways in which the writer uses space and the ways in which the painter, the draughtsman, the cartographer, etc. use space.

Nevertheless, the graphic devices available overlap, and overlap precisely because they are exploitations of the same basic resource – spatial relations. This overlap can be seen in the familar ways in which writing, drawing, etc. may not only share the same graphic surface but be semiologically related in virtue of sharing it (e.g. in book illustration, captions to photographs, etc.). Furthermore, one and the same graphic configuration can function simultaneously as a scriptorial sign and a pictorial sign. Illuminated initials in medieval manuscripts furnish an obvious example (Plate 1), and similar devices of graphic syncretism are widely exploited in modern advertising and fashion (Plate 2).

This elementary consideration points straight away to the conclusion that any viable discrimination in this area must appeal to specific features of the activities integrated. If this fails, then the distinction – in that instance – between writing and other forms of graphic communication collapses.

Distinguishing between the activities integrated will in many cases involve macrosocial as well as biomechanical factors. It is very evident, for example, that the techniques of the illustrator are quite different from those of the scribe. Although they may be combined in the expertise of one person, each demands a special training. Someone who learns to write may never learn to draw, and this fact cannot be offset or cancelled out by the success of those individuals who manage to do both.

Moreover, when we consider cases of graphic syncretism (Plate 1) from the point of view of anyone interpreting the message, it is evident that 'recognizing' the pictorial element involves quite different visual and mental processing from recognizing the scriptorial element (the letter form). Nor does recognition of the one automatically entail recognition of the other. This is another good reason, as far as the integrationist is concerned, for saying that in such cases we have two forms of communication combined, rather than postulating a separate single category of signs that are neither pictorial nor scriptorial. That is to say, the argument is that such cases can be analysed by relating the combined components severally to forms of communication which can – and do – exist independently. But that does *not* mean that it will be possible to resolve the graphic configuration itself into two separate sets of marks, colours, relations, etc., or divide the graphic space (Ch. 18) into two discrete areas allotted to the two forms of communication.

* * *

Reference was made earlier to another metaphysical premiss which is implicit in Saussurean semiology and may be taken up at this point. This is the Aristotelian premiss that the objects and events in time and space are the same for all (human) observers. Although it is never discussed by Saussure, this assumption clearly underlies the logic of the Saussurean 'circuit' of communication (Ch. 3). Otherwise, the circuit as described would give no guarantee that a linguistic community – or any other community of sign-users – is possible. That is to say, in order to be sure that what *A* says or writes can be identically understood by *both B and C* (not to mention *D, E, F* . . .), the Saussurean semiologist has to assume that – at least in the standard case – the spoken or written signs *A* produces are identically perceived by *B* and *C*; or, more exactly, that any perceptual variations between *B* and *C* fall below the threshhold which would make it possible to misidentify the sign. (But how the latter could be guaranteed short of an assurance of the former it is difficult to see.)

Integrational semiology does not need this premiss, and the reason why highlights what is perhaps the most fundamental theoretical divergence between integrational and Saussurean semiology. Unlike Saussurean semiology, integrational semiology does not construe communication in terms of shared identities.

Chapter 7

A theory of the written sign

Theories of the written sign will differ one from another according to the model of signification which they adopt. There are three main types of model for a semiologist to choose from: (i) *surrogational*, (ii) *structural*, and (iii) *integrational*.[1] In addition, these general models, which can be applied to other than written forms of communication, may be classified on the basis of a distinction between (iv) *fixed-code models* and *open models*.

1 *The surrogational model.* This is the oldest model of signification in the Western tradition. Its defining feature is that what a sign signifies is explained in terms of its being a surrogate or substitute for something else. As it is often put, the sign 'stands for' what it signifies. In order to interpret a sign correctly, therefore, we need to know what it stands for.

This abstract relation of 'standing for' something else is sufficiently general to allow application to many different types of case. Some of the applications are more 'literal' and some more 'metaphorical'. The chips used in a gambling casino are substitutes for money: they are purchased on entering and changed back into cash on leaving. In a strictly physical sense they take the place of money in the transactions that occur at the gambling tables. A different kind of substitution is involved if someone draws a diagram to explain how a machine works. Various lines and shapes in the diagram will stand for different parts of the machine, but they are not substitutes in any physical sense. The gardener who replaces his lawn mower by a diagram of a lawn mower will find that he has difficulty in cutting the grass. A scale model of the *Ark Royal*, although it may float in water and even sail, is not a craft that could be substituted for the *Ark Royal* in a naval engagement. Nevertheless, it might perfectly well stand for the *Ark Royal* in the reconstruction of some real or hypothetical naval engagement; or even in the making of a film. Japanese restaurants frequently display in the window plastic imitations of the dishes on offer, with appropriate price

---

1 For a fuller discussion, see R. Harris, 'Three models of signification', in H.S. Gill (ed.), *Structures of Signification*, vol. III (New Delhi: Wiley, 1993).

labels. This is not taken to mean either that the diner is expected to eat plastic, or that the plastic models are on sale at the prices indicated. A different kind of substitution is involved if, rather than delivering an oral message by telephone, I write a letter instead; and a different kind again if, instead of painting a cupboard, the artist paints the word *armoire* (Plate 9).

All these cases seem at least to have one feature in common: they involve a mental operation by which one thing is understood to be replaceable by another (and sometimes several simultaneous replacements are involved). What the replacement signifies is determined by what it replaces.

Signification is thus construed as a surrogational relation between the sign and something else. It is frequently described as a relation of 'representation'. The casino chips are said to represent money. The diagram represents the machine. Writing represents speech. Thus if we wish to understand what a sign signifies, we look for what it represents.

In a surrogational model of signification, there is no assumption that a sign has to resemble what it stands for. It would be perfectly possible to use a matchstick to represent the *Ark Royal*. But this would limit the representational purposes served by the substitution.

The surrogational model of signification is not a licence for deception either. Forging a ten-pound note is not, from a semiological perspective, the creation of a sign. On the contrary, the forger hopes that no one will be able to tell the difference between substitute and original: whereas this distinction is conceptually essential for the semiologist. *X* cannot 'stand for' *Y* if no one can tell *X* and *Y* apart.

Peirce, co-founder with Saussure of the modern study of signs, opted for a surrogational model of signification.

> A sign, or *representamen*, is something which stands to somebody for something in some respect or capacity. It addresses somebody, that is, creates in the mind of that person an equivalent sign, or perhaps a more developed sign. That sign which it creates I call the *interpretant* of the first sign. The sign stands for something, its *object*.[2]

2 *The structural model.* Surrogationalism seeks to explain signification in terms of relations between signs and what they stand for. The structural model, on the contrary, explains signification solely in terms of relations between signs and other signs.

Essential to this model is the notion that signs form systems. The system is envisaged as a structure which confers significance on all its constituent units. The paradigm example might be taken to be a currency system. The value of a ten-dollar note is internally ('systemically' or 'structurally')

2 J. Buchler (ed.), *Philosophical Writings of Peirce* (New York: Dover, 1955), p. 99.

connected to the value of a one-dollar note. Whatever those two values may be, they are not independent of each other.

This is a quite different notion of signification from that adopted in the surrogational model. The surrogational model is atomistic: it allows different signs to have different significations that are entirely unconnected, because each value is determined solely by what the individual sign 'stands for'. According to the structural model, the particular signification of any given sign will be a function of the similarities and differences which connect and contrast it with other signs in the same system.

As originally developed by Saussure, the structural model was specifically applied to languages, but it may be extended and adapted to deal with non-linguistic signs as well. For example, whether an irregular, unbroken black line on a map represents a river, a road, a railway or a national boundary is not something which is determined independently of the other carto-graphic conventions employed for the map in question. On the contrary, a cartographer who wishes to distinguish rivers from roads, roads from railways, and railways from national boundaries must necessarily choose different types of line in each case. If the cartographer fails to do so, then whatever his or her intentions may have been, the lines drawn on the map will be ambiguous. Thus, in terms of their signification, the conventions a cartographer uses form a structural complex in which the individual elements do not have meaning independently of the whole.

The structural model of signification is sometimes regarded as par-ticularly appropriate to the analysis of writing, inasmuch as writing is commonly conceived as involving the deployment of some traditionally organized system, such as the alphabet. Although there are different versions of the alphabet, we do not envisage it as an open-ended set of characters; nor as one in which the values of the letters *a*, *b*, *c*, etc. – whatever they may be – have nothing to do with one another. We assume, rather, that they are systematically contrastive units, which cannot be substituted for one another at random.

Saussure invokes the example of letter forms as a paradigm case to illustrate the structuralist principle that form depends on contrast within the system.[3] Pointing out that in the same individual's handwriting the letter *t* may appear in a variety of different shapes, Saussure claims that 'the one essential thing is that his *t* should be distinct from his *l*, his *d*, etc.'. In other words, the limits within which the form may vary are determined not by anything outside the system but by its internal structure, requiring *t* to contrast with the other letters of the alphabet.

3 *The integrational model.* The integrational model differs from the other two in being the only model to treat the sign as depending on the context in

3   F. de Saussure, *Cours de linguistique générale*, 2nd edn (Paris: Payot, 1922), p. 165.

which it is produced. An integrational semiology makes no assumption that the sign has any existence outside the communication situation that gives rise to it. Communication, for the integrationist, is the dynamic process in which signs are created.

The sign, therefore, is not to be confused with any corresponding abstraction recognized in a metalinguistic scheme (as in a dictionary, for example). The pervasiveness of this confusion is compounded by terminological failure to distinguish the two cases. The term *word*, for example, is commonly used, as Peirce pointed out, in (i) the sense in which there is only one word *daffodil* (in the English language), but also (ii) the sense in which there may be several words of this form on a single page. Printers count words in the latter sense, lexicographers in the former.

It is thus of crucial importance from an integrational point of view to distinguish between two uses of the term *sign*. In everyday parlance the word *sign* often refers to a physical object, as for instance in the advice to motorists given in the Highway Code to place a 'red warning sign (a reflecting triangle)' on the road at least 50 metres in front of a vehicle that has broken down. [4] This use of the word *sign* is a potential source of confusion. For the integrational theorist, the reflecting triangle does not become a sign until it is appropriately placed in a situation of the kind described. The same physical object – the red triangle – was not a sign during the time it remained in the boot of the motorist's car in readiness for such an emergency; nor, having once functioned as a sign, will it continue to do so when the motorist eventually puts it back in the boot again and proceeds on the journey. The spatio-temporal continuity of the object is irrelevant to its semiological role.

The implications of this for a theory of writing are important, as will become evident in subsequent chapters. But what may initially seem disconcerting is that it appears to conflict with certain traditional assumptions. As already pointed out, the permanence or at least the durability of the written text is often treated as one of its characteristic features. But if the sign functions only in a communicational context, does a text cease to be writing once the book is closed? The integrational approach might appear to sponsor a neo-Berkeleian scepticism about the existence of writing when there are no readers around.

To allay any such misapprehensions, it perhaps suffices here to make the following points.

First, the question is not whether the text ceases to be writing once the book is closed, but whether what guarantees written status is the spatio-temporal continuity of the marks through intermittent periods of invisibility. The case of a written text is different from that of a motorist's warning triangle, from an integrational point of view, precisely in that one

4   *The Highway Code*, rev. edn (London: HMSO, 1987), art. 133.

possible reason for having something written down is anticipation of the need to consult it later. It was noted in the previous chapter that ephemerality makes a difference to the range of human activities which signs can serve to integrate. But if durability *per se* is treated as the essential feature, then we are confusing the sign with its material manifestation. For while it is true that survival of any written text depends on the survival of some particular physical form of it, that is only a necessary and not a sufficient condition. A 'lost' text, such as Quintilian's treatise on the causes of the decline of oratory, is not lost because it somehow ceased to be writing, but because none of the copies has survived.

But a text can also be 'lost' because what the signs signify is no longer understood. It is here that the everyday use of the term *writing* may be misleading. No one stopped using the term *writing* to refer to Egyptian hieroglyphs, even though there was a period of several centuries during which all attempts to read them failed. The written texts were lost, although the hieroglyphic marks were preserved. Champollion's decipherment recovered the texts *as texts*, by creating a new class of potential readers.

In an integrational perspective, confusing survival of the hieroglyphic marks with survival of the hieroglyphic texts would be on a par with confusing the survival of Roman coins with the survival of Roman currency.

4 *Fixed-code and open models.* Individual signs are frequently envisaged as belonging to some established inventory of signs, as members of which they have a determinate form and meaning. Such inventories, which remain invariant with respect to the actual deployment of the individual signs from one occasion to the next, may be referred to as 'fixed codes'. This term does not imply that the inventories in question are not subject to change over the course of time, but rather that any alteration to the individual signs brings into existence a new inventory, which is semiologically independent of its predecessor.[5] (Thus 'change' is in effect envisaged as a chronological succession of separate fixed codes.)

Any model of signification which does not accord this priority to membership of an inventory, or which treats the inventory in question as not fixed (in the sense of having no determinate number of members) may be termed an 'open' model.

A surrogational model of signification may or may not also be a fixed-code model: there is no necessity that it should be. This is because what counts for the surrogationalist is the relationship between the individual sign and what it stands for. It makes no difference whether, for instance, the word *magenta* belongs to a given inventory of colour terms, for what

---

5 For the application of this concept to spoken languages, see R. Harris, 'On redefining linguistics', in H.G. Davis and T.J. Taylor (eds), *Redefining Linguistics* (London and New York: Routledge, 1990), pp. 29ff.

magenta signifies is determined by its correlation with a particular colour. But a structuralist model is automatically a fixed-code model, because it treats the signs as having no existence outside the particular system to which they belong. (Thus *magenta* has to contrast with words like *blue, purple, green,* etc.) An integrational model, on the other hand, is necessarily an open model, because its treats signification as deriving from the context, and not from membership of any invariant set of signs defined in advance. Hence for the integrationist what the word *magenta* signifies will depend on the particular contextual conditions that are relevant to its use on particular occasions.

Chapter 8

A theory of writing systems

A writing system, from an integrational point of view, exists as a set of (typically macrosocial) practices associated with an inventory of written forms. Acquaintance with such practices may constitute a resource for *A* and *B* in their written communication. In traditional writing systems, the practices are handed down from one generation to another and explicitly taught in educational curricula. But there are other writing systems than traditional ones.

According to Kroeber, to speak of a writing *system* already implies the acceptance of writing conventions and 'standardization':

> Conventionalization of form accompanies frequency or rapidity of writing, conventionalization of meaning must occur if there is to be any writing at all. It develops in pure non-phonetic pictography if this is to be able to express any considerable range of meaning. An outstretched hand may well be used with the sense of 'give.' But the beholder of the picture-writing is likely to interpret it as 'take.' Here is where conventionalization is necessary: it must be understood by writers and readers alike that such a hand means 'give' and not 'take,' or perhaps the reverse, or perhaps that if the palm is up and the fingers flat the meaning is 'give' whereas the palm below or the fingers half closed means 'take.' Whatever the choice, it must be adhered to; the standardized, conventional element has entered. That is why one customarily speaks of 'systems' of writing. Without the system, there can be not even picture-writing, but only pictures, whose range of power of communication is far more limited.[1]

From an integrational perspective, this insistence on conventionalization and uniformity of practice is misplaced. Indeed, if it were taken seriously there would be some difficulty in recognizing the existence of a writing system wherever (as, for instance, in the case of seventeenth-century English) individual writers are allowed to spell as they please. But if this

---

1 A.L. Kroeber, *Anthropology* (New York: Harcourt, Brace, 1923), p. 266.

Colour plates

Plate 1 Graphic syncretism in a medieval manuscript.

Plate 2 Graphic syncretism on a modern tee-shirt.

Plate 3 Palimpsest semantics.

Plate 4 Logographic tmesis.

Plate 5 Analogical uniformity: internal syntagmatics.

Plate 6 Analogical uniformity: external syntagmatics.

Plate 7 Anti-writing: Dada poster by Theo van Doesburg and Kurt Schwitters (1922).

latitude too is taken as part of the 'system', then conventionalization becomes too slippery a concept to be worth insisting on in the way Kroeber assumes. Nor is it easy to see why a form which can mean either 'give' or 'take', depending on the context, calls for clarification by 'conventionalization' if it is ever to achieve the status of being part of a writing *system*.

What seems to lie behind Kroeber's notion of writing systems is the construal of all communication systems as 'fixed codes' (Ch. 7) – and, ideally, fixed codes in which there is only one form for each meaning and only one meaning for each form.[2] For an integrationist, the term *system* has no such implications, and the idea that there can be no writing at all without the establishment of fixed inventories of standardized, unambiguous written forms is delusory.

A theory of writing systems, in the integrational sense, is concerned with the semiological differentiae which permit a typology of different kinds of writing to be constructed. This is not to be confused with giving an account of the process of *codification* by which, historically, different alphabets, syllabaries, etc. have emerged and been adopted in various parts of the world. These codified products are also commonly referred to as 'writing systems', but they are, from an integrational perspective, second-order constructs, and their codification is a social – and usually pedagogic – process which may take many centuries.

As already noted in Chapter 3, Saussure's theory of glottic scripts introduces a basic distinction between phonetic and non-phonetic writing. Non-phonetic writing systems are not further subdivided by Saussure, but phonetic writing systems are subdivided on the basis of the phonetic unit selected for representation. Thus we arrive at a typology which can be set out in the form of the following tree diagram:

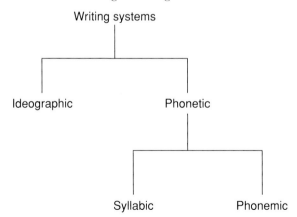

---

2 On the 'fixed code' fallacy, see R. Harris, *The Language Myth* (London: Duckworth, 1981), pp. 9–10.

Saussure's typology might be further extended. For instance, it would certainly be possible to have a phonetic script based on distinctive features rather than on phonemes. (Korean is sometimes cited as an example of such a system.[3])

A related but somewhat more elaborate theory of writing systems is proposed by Pulgram.[4] Pulgram distinguishes between seven different types of writing system, for which he proposes the terms (i) *pictorial*, (ii) *logographic*, (iii) *syllabic*, (iv) *alphabetic*, (v) *phonemic*, (vi) *phonetic* and (vii) *spectrographic*.

He hesitates over whether to class the first of his seven types as writing at all, since a pictorial system for him is one which utilizes 'a realistic picture' of some thing or situation. This leaves room for various possible renderings in speech (cf. Trager's very similar view, Ch.1). Pulgram comments:

> Were it not for the fact that . . . some true writing developed from the pictorial, one could just as well call it non-writing since it has little if anything in common with what customarily we understand writing to be.[5]

The *we* in this last sentence betrays the ethnocentric bias of Pulgram's approach. Evidently, systems which do not conform to 'our' assumptions are not to be regarded as true writing.

Pulgram's theory of scripts is more sophisticated than Saussure's in that, instead of a single *fundamentum divisionis*, he proposes a series of criteria to support his seven types. The relationship between these criteria and his typology of writing systems is set out in Table 8.1.

It will be noted that Saussure's theory of scripts is to all intents and purposes subsumed under Pulgram's column 5 ('Level').

A full critique of Pulgram's theory and an explanation of its terminology would require a discussion more detailed than is warranted in the present context, for in the end Pulgram's foundational assumption does not differ from Saussure's. In effect, writing (or at least 'true' writing) is equated by Pulgram with the representation of speech. All the subdivisions of his typology are reflections of the various ways in which this representation can be achieved, and it is clear that Pulgram's theory could not even begin to accommodate writing systems devised for recording non-auditory activities of any kind.

From the viewpoint adopted in integrational semiology, the mistake inherent in systematizations of the kind proposed by Saussure and Pulgram is the tacit assumption that the structure of a writing system is established simply by correlating its graphic units with units of some non-written

---

3 G. Sampson, *Writing Systems* (London: Hutchinson, 1985), Ch. 7. The same author also cites Pitman's shorthand as an example of a 'featural' writing system.
4 E. Pulgram, 'The typologies of writing-systems', in W. Haas (ed.), *Writing Without Letters* (Manchester: Manchester University Press, 1976), pp. 1–28.
5 *Ibid.*, p. 10.

Table 8.1

Typologies

1 System	2 Evolution	3 Code	4 Communication	5 Level	6 Graph	7 Signal	8 Script
pictorial	pre-writing	praeter-glottic	semasio-graphic	utterance	pictographic	sign	illustrative
logographic	→			word	logographic		orthographic
syllabic			glotto-graphic	syllable	syllabo-graphic		
alphabetic	writing	glottic		sound	phono-graphic	figura	
phonemic							transcrip-tional
phonetic							
spectro-graphic							

medium. Thus when these correlations have been identified and any substitutions, equivalences or combinatorial restrictions duly noted, the description of the writing system is complete.

This is not the assumption of the integrational semiologist, for whom this would amount simply to projecting on to writing the structure of some non-written system (usually speech). For the integrationist, the written sign is a contextual product, and accordingly systems of writing will differ from one another as a function of the various types of activity they integrate. It is to be expected that some differences will be manifest in the utilization of graphic space, others in the inventory of graphic forms deployed.

One result of this is that what theorists like Saussure and Pulgram would count as one and the same script may for the integrationist be two different scripts. In effect, both Saussure and Pulgram identify a writing system with the linguist's analysis of the way a given spoken language is translated into a repertory of graphic units. What this leaves out of account is the fact that readers of an English or a Latin or a Greek text need to know much more than the language it is written in. At the very least, they need to grasp also certain principles governing relevant scanning procedures. For the integrationist, this is an essential part of the reading process, i.e. of the activities integrated, and the rationale for this is the simple fact that an application of the wrong scanning procedures can render the written text incomprehensible.

Consequently, from an integrational point of view, the writing system employed, for example, in a boustrophedon text is necessarily different from the writing system employed in any non-boustrophedon text, even though the alphabet employed and the 'verbal content' of the two texts may be in a linguist's eyes exactly the same.

A more dramatic and perhaps more controversial illustration of the same point is provided by the following example:

(i) Lord, who createdst man in wealth and store, though foolishly he lost the same, decaying more and more, till he became most poore: with thee O let me rise as larks, harmoniously, and sing this day thy victories: then shall the fall further the flight in me. My tender age in sorrow did beginne: and still with sicknesses and shame thou didst so punish sinne that I became most thinne. With thee let me combine and feel this day thy victorie: for, if I imp my wing on thine, affliction shall advance the flight in me.

Word for word, this is George Herbert's poem 'Easter wings'. In many modern editions it appears as:

(ii)

Lord, who createdst man in wealth and store,
Though foolishly he lost the same,
Decaying more and more,
Till he became
Most poore:
With   thee
O let me rise
As   larks,   harmoniously,
And sing this day thy victories:
Then shall the fall further the flight in me.

My   tender   age   in   sorrow   did   beginne:
And still with sicknesses and shame
Thou didst so punish sinne,
That I became
Most thinne.
With   thee
Let me combine
And feel this day thy victorie:
For, if I imp my wing on thine,
Affliction shall advance the flight in me.

But as originally published, on facing pages, it read:

(iii)

¶ Easter wings.

¶ Easter wings.

Lord, who createdst man in wealth and store,
Though foolishly he lost the same,
Decaying more and more,
Till he became
Most poore:
With thee
O let me rise
As larks, harmoniously,
And sing this day thy victories:
Then shall the fall further the flight in me

My tender age in sorrow did beginne
And still with sicknesses and shame
Thou didst so punish sinne,
That I became
Most thinne.
With thee
Let me combine,
And feel this day thy victorie:
For, if I imp my wing on thine,
Affliction shall advance the flight in me.

Discussing this poem, one critic points out that the modern reader is apt to judge Herbert's presentation of it to be original but 'over-ingenious'.[6] Such a reaction, he suggests, is largely the result of modern unfamiliarity with the long history of pattern poetry. (The 'wings' image was used in the sixteenth century by Melin de Saint-Gelais and goes back to Simias of Rhodes at the beginning of the third century BC.) But it may also be regarded as reflecting the pervasive logocentrism (in Derrida's sense) of the European tradition, which depreciates all aspects of writing that cannot be treated as a direct reflection of the spoken word.

The point here is not simply that version (i) conceals the verse structure, whereas versions (ii) and (iii) exhibit it, nor that (ii) defeats Herbert's purpose by failing to represent the bird as rising; but that all three versions utilize the graphic space available so as to require the reader to scan the texts in quite different ways.

Any reader who failed to realize this, and so read (ii) as if it were written in exactly the same way as (i), would miss entirely the poet's iconographic image of the wings, as well as the verbo-visual puns (*Decaying more and more, Most thinne*, etc.); while a reader who read (iii) similarly (i.e. failed even to grasp the necessity of rotating the printed page through 90 degrees between scanning the title and scanning the lines) would presumably have a hard time making anything of the poem at all.

For an integrationist, (i), (ii) and (iii) exemplify different writing systems; whereas for most traditional theorists they exemplify one and the same system.

Insisting on this difference between (i), (ii) and (iii) will doubtless seem pernickety to many; but that is because Western education teaches one to identify the 'writing system' as the traditional second-order construct, implicitly defined on the basis of the alphabet used and the language represented, but ignoring everything else. In fact, nothing could be more *systematic* than the requirement to change the orientation of the page at specific points in the scanning of the text. The writer imposes this requirement on the reader by the way he has chosen to use the graphic space at his disposal. And this freedom, from an integrational perspective, is of the essence of writing, because writing is not reducible to the use of a fixed code.

Thus it would be a mistake to dismiss the above example as a case of 'poetic licence' which has nothing to do with writing *as such*. It is possible to find examples in which the kind of device Herbert exploits has become

6   D. Higgins, *George Herbert's Pattern Poems: In Their Tradition* (New York: Unpublished Editions, 1977), p. 4. The word 'over-ingenious' is quoted from Helen Gardner's introduction to her edition of Herbert's poems (London: Oxford University Press, 1961). Gardner in fact prints the text in format (ii), as if to dissociate herself from those who find Herbert's aesthetics 'over-ingenious', while at the same time not condoning entirely the unwonted liberties taken by the poet with the rectitude of the English printed page.

a uniform feature. Such examples abound in mathematical and musical writing. To read

$$24 + 12 = 36$$

we need a different scanning procedure from that needed for reading

$$\begin{array}{r} 24 \\ 12 \\ \hline 36 \end{array}$$

even though the mathematical proposition expressed is in both cases the same. Similarly, exactly the same melody can be expressed in a simple sequence of alphabetic letters as in a configuration of notes displayed on a stave; but the two scripts involved are semiologically quite different.

Taking an integrational approach thus opens up the possibility of a typology of writing systems which cuts across the traditional division between glottic and non-glottic writing altogether and focuses instead on similarities and differences between the ways in which various kinds of writing utilize the graphic space available. The theoretical justification for this change of emphasis is that the utilization of graphic space, and its implications for processing the text, may be factors common to many forms of writing *irrespective* of whether the signs are to be interpreted phonetically, logographically, musically, etc. It thus takes higher priority than any typology based simply on what kind of information the unit signs of a given system record.

Since, in any case, there is no limit to the kind of information that writing can handle, an information-based typology will eventually be no more enlightening than a mere list of everything human beings might want to communicate about; whereas an integrationally based typology will at least show how the mind tackles the problem of using spatial configurations to bridge the gap between biomechanically diverse activities.

Chapter 9

Forming, processing and interpretation

From an integrational point of view, the writer is no more to be thought of merely as the 'sender' of a written message than the reader is to be thought of merely as its 'receiver'. The whole sender/receiver model of communication is unacceptable. It already involves a question-begging abstraction, by which the message is conjured into existence as a third entity, regardless of whether anyone actually sends it or receives it. This requires us to view communication not as a function of the interaction between *A* and *B*, but as the transmission of an object. The object, as an independent fact, then becomes as essential to the explication of communication between *A* and *B* as a tennis ball does to any account of how *A* and *B* play tennis.

In an integrational account of communication, there is no semiological tennis ball. But this lacuna encounters deeply entrenched resistance in the case of writing. Do we not actually *send* letters to one another? Is it not the case that sometimes they arrive and sometimes they do not? How would this be possible if the message did not exist in its own right as a transmittable object? That there is such an object might even seem to be a presupposition of writing itself. In Old Babylonian, the customary form for letters ran: 'Please Mr A, Mr B sends the following message.'[1] Then follows 'the message'.

From an integrational point of view, these are puzzles only for those who have already confused the written sign with the document. The creation of a written sign involves the contextualized integration of a number of complementary activities. We can distinguish various semiologically relevant aspects of these activities, if we wish, by separating out *forming* and *processing* from *interpretation*. But if we do so, it is important to stress that these are not separate stages on some conveyor belt along which 'the message' is passed.

The difference between forming and processing partially corresponds to that implied by the contrast between the traditional terms *writing* and *reading*, but is of broader scope. Forming is to be taken to include any activity or sequence of activities by means of which a written form is produced, and

---

1   C.B.F. Walker, *Cuneiform* (London: British Museum, 1987), p. 27.

processing to include any activity or sequence of activities by means of which the written form is then examined for purposes of interpretation. (*Processing* is preferable to *scanning* as a general term, since the latter might be taken to imply restriction to processing by sight. This is obviously unsatisfactory for writing in general: a braille or Moon-type text presupposes tactile processing, not visual processing.)

That the theoretical recognition of processing is not merely an artifact of integrational analysis is obvious to anyone who has ever been called upon to do proof-reading. Proof-reading requires a different scanning technique from that which one normally uses for reading; and that is why it is so easy to miss typographical errors. But it would be a mistake to suppose that the difference is merely that one is called upon to read more 'carefully' (whatever that might mean). Proof-reading involves the integration of different activities and the application of different criteria from those relevant to the ordinary reading of a text. It aims at a different kind of interpretation.

Forming a written message does not have to involve scoring a surface or leaving traces upon it: the formation might consist of arranging a set of free-standing objects, or showing a pattern of coloured lights, or even planting flowers to grow in certain configurations.

Forming and processing do not necessarily have to involve physiologically different types of activity. It might be possible, for instance, to produce a device for handicapped people with impaired vision in which 'reading' involved retracing the written marks by means of a hand-held automatic stylus. In such a case, forming and processing would involve essentially the same movements.

The semiology of writing will rarely, if ever, have occasion to be concerned with a comprehensive analysis of the biomechanics involved in forming, processing and interpretation. The concern of the semiologist is focused on the area where the activities of forming, processing and interpretation intermesh to create the written sign. The judgment involved in interpreting the written message may indeed relate back to its formation, as well as forward to future activities anticipated. That reference to a temporal continuum of activities – as already noted (Ch. 5) – is implicit in the integrational concept of writing, as of all other modes of communication.

Processing involves (i) recognizing certain units, and (ii) recognizing the patterns into which these units are organized for purposes of articulating the message. It already goes beyond mere inspection or sensory apprehension. It is possible to look at a text without processing it, let alone interpreting the written message.

But although processing anticipates interpretation, it does not automatically lead to it. A document can be scanned but not understood, for any one of many possible reasons. The question is sometimes debated whether the term *reading* can properly be applied to any process which stops short of comprehension of the written message. The oral performance commonly called 'reading aloud' can certainly be executed correctly by someone who does not understand the words being read. But it could not be executed either correctly or incorrectly without going through what is here designated by the term *processing*. In the terminology we shall adopt, reading a text aloud could itself constitute one type of interpretation, irrespective of whether the reader understood what was being read. Similarly, writing something down could count as interpretation (as in the case of a scribe copying out a text in an unfamiliar foreign language). Thus neither processing nor interpreting necessarily entails understanding the text, at least in the sense in which 'understanding' is commonly taken. Someone might be able to both scan and pronounce correctly (i.e. orally interpret) a written notice that says *Danger de mort*, but fail to understand the message because of a defective knowledge of French.

It will be evident from what has already been said that, from an integrational point of view, reading as such is not to be equated with transposition from one sensory mode to another (i.e. reading aloud). The confusion is part and parcel of the Saussurean approach to writing, where it is assumed that the written word exists only to represent the spoken word. It is also supported by everyday metalinguistics, in which the verb *read* is often used in the sense of 'pronounce aloud'. But if this equation were valid, reading would be forever beyond the reach of the congenitally mute.

A similar confusion consists in regarding reading as a kind of mental verbalization, in which written signs are translated into silent speech.

For the integrationist, reading does not correspond to any precisely definable activity or set of activities. Reading a novel is something quite different from reading a musical score, just as writing a novel is different from writing a symphony. In both cases, however, the sign is the mechanism which integrates the activities involved.

The area where forming, processing and interpretation converge cannot be further defined in general terms, except to say that it is the area in which non-kinetic spatial configurations, the products of the forming activity, are meaningfully organized. Where that area is located can perhaps best be explained by taking a specific example, which will also illustrate the integrational principle that the written sign depends on the activities integrated.

In Classical Tibetan, sequences of written forms are segmented by the occurrence of small dots (see Fig. 9.1 opposite). As analysed by Beyer,[2] each *tsheg-bar* (= 'between the dots') is a space within which various positions may be distinguished. These are arranged as indicated in the following diagram:

---

2   S.V. Beyer, *The Classical Tibetan Language* (Albany: State University of New York Press, 1992), pp. 42ff.

```
                      5
                      2
            1         3        6        7
                      4
                      5
```

The minimum *tsheg-bar* comprises a mark occupying position 3; the next-to-minimum is a mark occupying position 3 plus another occupying one of the two positions numbered 5; and so on. There are twenty-nine different marks to choose from for position 3, but the inventory of marks that can occur in the other positions is more restricted: for instance, only five can occur in position 1 and only three in position 2.

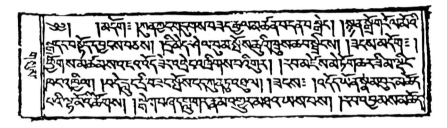

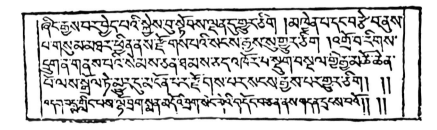

Figure 9.1 Tibetan writing

The numbers assigned to the various positions in Beyer's analysis correspond to an 'order' in which the marks are arranged. This order is not evident from the visual configuration itself, but is based on the correspondence between each *tsheg-bar* and a phonetic syllable in the spoken Classical language. The order in fact corresponds to the order of the various consonants and vowels. Thus knowing the order, plus knowing the phonology of Classical Tibetan, enables the reader to give the syllable in question its Classical pronunciation.

Is the order within the *tsheg-bar* (as analysed above) an element of the written sign in Tibetan? From an integrational point of view, the answer depends on the activity or activities taken to be involved in interpretation, i.e. the activity or activities that complete the integrational process. According to Beyer, all Tibetan reading is reading aloud.[3] However, modern pronunciation is not that of Classical Tibetan: e.g. what are still written today in Classical Tibetan as three different forms corresponding phonologically to <sgrub>, <bsgrubs> and <bsgrub> will be identically pronounced by a reader in Lhasa (as *tup*, with a retroflex *t*). It follows that if the interpretation process is posited to be the identification of the original pronunciation lying behind the Classical spellings, then indeed an acquaintance with the order is relevant to the correct interpretation of the written signs. But it seems clear that there must be many Tibetan readers who have little idea of how the Classical language was pronounced, and do not need to know this in order to read the texts. For such readers the activity of interpretation is necessarily different, and the order of marks in the *tsheg-bar* will not signify for them what it presumably signified for readers of a previous age.

The result of divergences between Classical phonology and modern pronunciation, as Beyer points out,[4] is not only that Tibetans are 'terrible spellers' but that, although literate, they can say things that they do not know how to write at all.

From an integrational point of view, therefore, the written sign is not to be equated with the written form. It is not only that different interpretations may require different processing procedures. Even if the processing procedure is the same, different activities of interpretation may confer different significations on the same set of marks. Thus in music, for example, the same configuration of notes on a stave will mean different things when interpreted in terms of the playing of two quite different instruments.

3   *Ibid.*, p. 52.
4   *Ibid.*, p. 40.

Part II

Topics in the theory of the written sign

Chapter 10

Signs, emblems and tokens

Writing as we know it today, like many other forms of communication, would be impossible if human beings were incapable of distinguishing between (i) *tokens* and (ii) *emblems*.

Tokens are signs based on one–one correlations between single items. Emblems are signs based on one–many correlations, in virtue of which the 'many' are regarded as forming a single class.

Communication between human beings would manifestly be a different enterprise altogether if we could not grasp this basic distinction (i.e. if we could not grasp, for example, that two Union Jacks do not identify two different countries, but one and the same country, whereas two notches on a tally stick do indeed signify two separate items to be counted).

Emblems obey the logic of replication: ideally, a given emblem always takes the same form. Tokens obey the logic of cumulation: what matters is not that tokens should be alike or different, but that they should be discrete and denumerable.

The shipwrecked sailor who scratches another stroke on the tree trunk with his knife every morning in order to keep count of the number of days he has spent on his desert island is using a token-iterative method of recording the passage of time.

'But is he writing?' someone may ask. To which the integrationist's answer is that it is not the purpose of integrational analysis to arbitrate on the usage of the word *writing*. The integrationist's aim is to analyse the semiological mechanisms of certain forms of communication. What can certainly be said is that the sailor is using a set of spatially organized marks to integrate past, present and possible future activities – and this is the basic function that writing serves. By using the marks in this way, the sailor secures an intellectual grasp of his own situation in time that he would not otherwise have. But the integrationist will also point out that it would make no difference whether the sailor carved a different letter of the alphabet each day instead of a simple notch. Nor indeed if he carved nothing, but merely added one more pebble to a pile of pebbles set aside for that purpose. All these forms of record-keeping would be, in this context, communicationally equivalent in the sense of being token-based. A token is defined not by its material form but by its semiological function.

A record-keeping programme of this kind involves the integration of two separate activities. The sailor, having carved the tokens on the tree trunk, has to go through a second procedure – counting them – whenever he wishes to know *how many* days he has been there. These activities, although biomechanically distinct, are integrationally inseparable. The sailor might eventually, for instance, become too weak through lack of food to use his knife effectively, but nevertheless remain quite capable of counting the marks already made. However, his ability to count becomes useless as soon as he is physically unable to continue using his knife.

It does not matter *in which order* the sailor counts the tokens he has made, provided that he counts no token twice, nor omits any. But it is necessary that each token be distinct from its neighbours in order to be countable at all. Correspondingly, in making the marks he does not have to follow any particular sequence, but he must not forget to make a mark each morning, nor by mistake make two marks on the same day. Provided he keeps to these simple rules, his reckoning will be accurate.

Written numeral signs in many cultures reflect the practice of token-iterative counting. The first three Roman numeral figures (I, II, III) are clearly token-iterative in form, as are the first three in Chinese and the first nine in Sumerian cuneiform.

In more sophisticated forms of communication, the contrast between tokens and emblems is often blurred by the fact that a sign functioning as emblem or token may also have other semiological functions as well. Nevertheless, the basic distinction may be illustrated by citing some relatively uncomplicated examples.

1 *Emblems.* Typical emblems include signatures, proper names, masons' marks, potters' seals, manufacturers' labels, logos, trademarks and national flags. The common semiological factor in these cases is the identification of one particular *X* – and no other – across all the range of instances in which the emblem occurs. It follows from this that a primary requirement for a sign to function effectively as an emblem is that it should, in principle, not be open to confusion with any other emblem likely to occur in the same context. (Individuals with the same name or companies with the same logo run the risk of being mistaken for one another.) It also follows that however often the emblem is replicated, it remains in principle associated with the same *X*. Thus the emblem functions as a semiological constant, whereas the token functions as a non-specific variable.

2 *Tokens.* Typical tokens include notches on a tally stick, some kinds of admission ticket, counters in certain board games, beads on an abacus, ticks or crosses on a list, and – in some contexts – pronouns such as *another*. The

common semiological factor in these cases is the availability of the sign to correlate with any one of an indefinite number of new items, without identifying the item in question other than as a separate unit. We are not so much concerned in such cases with *which* individual item corresponds to which individual token: what matters is that the total number in a set of such tokens should correspond to the total number of items recorded, inventoried or classified. It follows that the mathematics of tokens is in effect just the opposite of the mathematics of emblems, where, as noted above, more occurrences of the same form do *not* indicate an increase in the number of items signified.

For the integrationist, both emblems and tokens relate to the way our experience of the world is structured by the passage of time. That is to say, the difference between them is in turn based on a more fundamental ability, which is being able to tell the difference between (i) persons, things, places, etc. familiar from previous encounters and (ii) others not previously encountered. Our reliance on the ability to distinguish old from new permeates every aspect of our experience and our understanding of the world around us.

From an integrational point of view, this differentiation is crucial because it underlies all basic communicational strategies. Emblems are signs which reflect recognition of 'the same X again', while tokens are signs which reflect recognition of 'another (different) X'.[1] Without such a distinction, communication would be very poorly adapted to the spatial and temporal organization of the human environment. We need 'same again' signs as well as 'different' signs, because we have to live in a world where two things cannot occupy the same physical space at the same time, but the same thing can occupy the same space at various times, and no one can keep track of everything continuously.

Consequently we can sometimes be mistaken in applying the distinction. We may fail to recognize an old acquaintance, and we may occasionally think we have already done a task that is yet to be done. But people who consistently fail to recognize the familiar, or lose a sense of time completely, are generally considered pathological cases whose disability unfits them for leading a normal existence. It certainly makes communication with them very difficult.

Nor, apart from such cases, is applying the distinction always problem-free. A girl is easily mistaken for her twin sister: we may be puzzled to know

---

1 Unfortunately, everyday usage of the words *same* and *different* rides roughshod over an important distinction, i.e. between cases where the 'same' X is spatio-temporally continuous and cases where it is not. In one sense, Manchester United's 3–0 defeat this week is not 'the same result again' as their 3–0 defeat last week. The score was the same, and they may even have fielded the same team, but there were two results, not one. Nor is having fish and chips for supper on consecutive nights a case of the 'same X again' in this sense, since two meals were consumed, not one meal twice.

whether the twin we are now addressing is the one we met this morning. At some distant point in the remote past, it must doubtless have puzzled our ancestors to know whether it was the same moon that appeared every night in the sky or a succession of different moons. But such puzzles would make no sense for creatures incapable of distinguishing 'the same X again' from 'another X'.

Any society whose members were in general deficient in this respect would never develop any common system of time reckoning nor, more basically, any agreed system of counting at all, let alone be able to communicate specific information about times and quantities. From the fact that all known societies do have some system of time reckoning and some system of quantification, it is a reasonable inference that we are dealing here with a universal human ability. This, at least, is what the integrationist assumes. In other words, integrational theory does not supply any further explanation or analysis of this ability, but takes it as a common foundation for all forms of human communication.

The difference between emblems and tokens reflects only one aspect of this more general ability. But it answers to quite different programmes for the formation, processing and interpretation of signs. In no form of communication do we treat tokens in the same way as emblems. To mistake a token for an emblem or vice versa is, in most cases, to misunderstand the message, or else to fail to make sense of it at all.

Our understanding of signs as emblems or tokens cannot be divorced from our more general understanding of the context in which they occur. For instance, in maps of the type found in a school atlas we should be perplexed to find a country called 'Belgium' marked twice on the same map, but not surprised to find it on two separate maps on different pages. But there is no general semiological principle which prohibits an artist from representing the same places, persons and objects more than once in the same picture. To fail to recognize such instances would be no less of a misunderstanding than to take the atlas as showing the existence of several countries called 'Belgium'.

An interesting example is provided by a petroglyph recorded by School-craft and discussed by Tylor (Fig. 10.1[2]).

This, allegedly, records an expedition across Lake Superior, led by a chief depicted on horseback with his magical drumstick in his hand. There were fifty-one men in five canoes, the first of them being led by the chief's ally, whose name, Kishkemunazee ('Kingfisher') is shown by a drawing of this bird. The land-tortoise indicates that the canoes reached the other side. The three suns under the three skies mean that the crossing took them three days.

---

2   E.B. Tylor, *Anthropology* (London: Macmillan, 1881), Ch. VII.

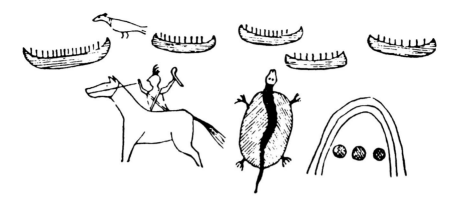

Figure 10.1 Emblem-token duplication.

If the above interpretation is correct,[3] the artist is utilizing the distinction between tokens and emblems in a quite sophisticated way. The chief and his ally Kingfisher must have crossed the lake with the rest, but we cannot pick them out among the fifty-one little matchstick-men tokens in the canoes. However, as befits their status in the expedition, their presence is also recorded by the figure on the horse and the bird. So in effect these two leaders are given dual representation in the picture: once as anonymous members of the company of fifty-one Indians, and once as individuals identified by their appropriate emblems. Each is represented by a token (as just 'another Indian') and also emblematically as a specific person.

Emblems and tokens may be of the most diverse kinds. In general, the form of a token matters less than the form of an emblem. This is because, as noted above, the emblem has to identify 'the same X' over and over again. With tokens, on the other hand, it often makes no difference whether we use a stroke, a tick, a cross, a dash, or some other mark: any of these, in principle, will serve as tokens. With tokens what usually matters more is exactly *where* the mark is placed. Is the tick opposite *this* entry on the list, or the entry above? Does the cross on the chart record the patient's temperature as 97 degrees or 98?

Likewise, there is in principle no limit to the variety of items that one kind of token can record. The Nootka Indians are reported to have used knots on a string to keep a count of such varied things as the passage of lunar months, the number of times a particular bathing ritual had been

---

3 A somewhat different interpretation of the same petroglyph is given by I.J. Gelb in *A Study of Writing* (Chicago: University of Chicago Press, 1952; rev. edn 1963), pp. 29–30.

performed, how many sea otters a hunter had killed, how many days a trip had taken and how many days a pubescent girl had spent in restriction.[4] Diversity of function and simplicity of form are, in general, the semiological hallmarks of the token.

In certain contexts, however, both the form and the place of the token may be rigidly prescribed. A cross – not a tick – must be placed in the square printed on the ballot form. But that does not elevate the cross itself from a token into an emblem. In some circumstances, the form of the token matters even more: one may be required to use one's whole body as a token, as when, for instance, voting is conducted by walking in person into a division lobby. Here the token *is* the voter, and the vote is not valid unless the (duly qualified) voter is present at the right place and the right time. But that still does not make the token an emblem. For all the specificity, it is just 'another vote'.

The simplest form of message based entirely on the token is a message which says, in effect: 'One more of these (whatever they are).' It thereby, indirectly, adds a new item to the set of 'these' being taken account of. Correspondingly, the simplest form of message based entirely on the emblem is one which says: 'Here is the sign of *X*.' It thereby, indirectly, usually indicates the owner, maker, proprietor, designer, etc. of the item to which the sign is attached.

But the archetypal emblem and the archetypal token are manifestly very restricted types of semiological device. Are they of any special importance in writing?

The integrational answer to this question requires a further distinction to be recognized. A sign may function *simultaneously* both as emblem and as token. Signs with this dual function we may call *duplex* signs.

Let us suppose the shipwrecked sailor decides to keep a rough record of the weather on his island. With this end in view, he marks a simple horizontal stroke on his tree-trunk record for each dry day, but a horizontal stroke with a bar across it for each day it rains. His system is still token-iterative, but there are two new semiological features. In the first place, if he wishes to know how long ago it last rained, he must start putting the marks in identifiable chronological order – something that was unnecessary as long as all the information he wished to record was how long he had been on the island. In the second place, he is now keeping a count of two different kinds of day – dry days and wet days. So his tokens are also functioning as emblems. Each emblem is correlated with a different meteorological category – 'dry' versus 'wet' – and that is why he now needs two formally differentiated marks instead of a simple stroke. His signs are duplex signs.

From an integrational point of view, the move from a simple token-iterative

---

4   W.J. Folan, 'The calendrical and numerical systems of the Nootka', in M.P. Closs (ed.), *Native American Mathematics* (Austin: University of Texas Press, 1986), p. 106.

system to a duplex system is important because the activities integrated have now become more complex. A new source of potential error has arisen; for it is no longer sufficient to be able to go through the biomechanical procedures required (cutting the strokes and counting them): it has become essential to *both* procedures to remember *which series is which*. In effect, this imposes a higher-order biomechanical requirement, subsuming the two basic requirements but not being entailed by either or both.

The paradigm case in contemporary society is currency. All currency systems obey both the logic of replication and the logic of cumulation. Every coin in circulation is a duplex sign. Even the traveller abroad, struggling with an unfamiliar currency, will automatically assume that any two coins of identical form have the same value, while coins of different shapes and sizes are likely to have different values. Thus two identical coins will be worth twice as much as one, three will be worth three times as much, and so on.

Our recognition of the status of duplex signs is manifest in our behaviour with respect to money. If we acquire two identical coins, we do not throw one away, as we might in the case of two identical copies of today's newspaper. 'I have another one' is a reason which makes sense when disposing of the newspaper, but if offered when throwing away a coin must be treated either as a joke or as a symptom of mental disturbance.

Writing falls into the category of communication that makes systematic use of duplex signs, although the logic of replication and cumulation is not as rigorously applied as in the case of currency. Nevertheless, for the integrationist the availability of duplex signs is important because duplex signs make it possible to integrate different activities – and in a different way – from any form of communication based on emblems or tokens only. In the case of written communication, this emerges most clearly in the imposition of different processing strategies on the reader. For example, a directory which lists

NELSON, Demetria
NELSON, Duane
NELSON, Gary
NELSON, Heather Jean
NELSON, Holly Cristin
NELSON, Katherine Eli
NELSON, Laura
NELSON, Margaret

requires us to read the orthographic form NELSON as having a dual function. The number of its occurrences corresponds to the number of persons listed: hence the sign functions as a token. It also functions as an emblem, distinguishing this group of individuals from other groups in the directory with different surnames.

It is worth noting, for comparison, that the same information might be given in the following form:

NELSON, Demetria
        Duane
        Gary
        Heather Jean
        Holly Cristin
        Katherine Eli
        Laura
        Margaret

In this second list NELSON is not read as a duplex sign: it functions as an emblem, but not as a token. Its single occurrence identifies a single name-class. Nevertheless, the two lists record the same facts. This is possible because other features of the second document (the listing arrangement of the written forms) allow for recording the information that all eight individuals share the same surname. But if it were necessary to print name-cards for these individuals to wear at a conference or reception, the procedure adopted in the second list would not be viable: i.e. if only Demetria Nelson had her name in full on her card and the other Nelsons simply had their first names. (This might conceivably happen if the job were entrusted to an illiterate office boy who did not understand how to read a list of the second type. His error would be an example of emblem/token confusion.)

It might perhaps be argued that in the second list the sign NELSON is 'invisibly repeated' or 'understood' at the beginning of each of the last seven lines. But this is tantamount to insisting on describing the second list as a truncated version of the first. One might equally – but with no better semiological justification – insist on describing the first list as a needlessly amplified version of the second. The fact is that two different semiological devices are used in the two cases, neither can be 'reduced to' the other, and each list consequently requires a different processing strategy from the reader.

The point illustrated above is a very general one: the function of a sign as emblem or token is connected with the overall organization of semiological space in a particular context.

Duality of function – the use of duplex signs – is found in all culturally important forms of writing that have emerged so far in history. But it is not a historical reason which dictates its recognition as a characteristic feature of writing. The semiological rationale is that graphic communication by means of duplex signs gives rise to a syntagmatics which distinguishes it from those forms of graphic communication in which duplex signs are not available. For instance, the score of a piano sonata, a page of mathematical equations and a chapter of a modern novel share certain features of graphic organization which depend on their use of duplex signs. In fact, if graphic communication had remained restricted to signs that functioned *either* as emblems *or* as tokens, there would be no musical scores, no mathematical equations and no novels – at least, not in the familiar forms in which they make their appearance in modern writing.

Integrational theory also offers an explanation of this preference for duplex signs. The reason is one of communicational economy. Writing which systematically excluded duplex signs would require a quite different (and in most cases more cumbersome) organization of graphic space (Ch. 18). Duality of function makes it possible to express lengthy messages in a relatively compact way, while not adding unduly to the complexity of inscription or interpretation.

However, where textual compactness would be a hindrance to communication rather than an advantage, we find the development of forms of writing which allow the emblematic function and the token function to be separated out. This is done systematically in certain kinds of musical notation (Ch. 21).

Chapter 11

The signature

The signature, in some ways the most intriguing 'sign of writing' ever evolved, is a paradigm case of the emblem (Ch. 10). Its existence provides a crucial test case for all theories of the written sign.

Any serious consideration of the signature immediately throws into relief the inadequacy of the claim that writing is simply a substitute for speech. For here there is no corresponding speech act. (Introducing or identifying oneself by name in speech is something quite different.)

The semiological status of the signature is explained from an integrational point of view as deriving from the unique series of activities which a signature integrates. These vary macrosocially from culture to culture, and even, within the same culture, according to circumstantial factors. Nevertheless, all written forms of signature share certain semiological features, regardless of whether the biomechanics of signing involve using a pen, seal, rubber stamp or any other piece of equipment.

Central to this integrational role is the feature that its formation – the signing itself – *identifies* the signatory (at least, in the typical or ideal case). In other words, the signature depends on a crucial semiological relationship obtaining between (i) the specific individual in question, (ii) the specific biomechanical act of signing, and (iii) the specific form produced. This is true of no other written sign. But it is true of the signature in all its many guises, including those that are not traditionally regarded as 'written' – such as the thumbprint (accepted in some parts of the world as equivalent to a name-signature and having the same legal force[1]).

The modern signature shows the emblematic sign carried to its logical conclusion. But, paradoxical though it may appear at first, the signature, *qua* written sign, cannot be explained by reference to any writing system. And this emerges most clearly when we consider the current Western practice, as

---

1 In the first millennium BC the thumbnail imprint was accepted as valid in Mesopotamia, and in Old Babylonian impressing the hem of one's garment on the edge of a tablet served the same purpose. See C.B.F. Walker, *Cuneiform* (London: British Museum, 1987), p. 26.

in the signing of cheques, letters, wills, arms reduction treaties, etc. For, quite literally, in these cases there is no question of being taught to sign one's name. It is not a mere extension of being taught to write. Writing systems are taught by means of models. But for the modern signature there is no model. Nor could there be. No such model is either empirically or logically possible. No one else can sign your name for you. Nor can you, by inspecting someone else's signature, learn what yours is.

It is tempting to try to construct counterexamples to undermine this thesis. But the attempt in the end is both self-defeating and revealing. Suppose, for instance, young Prince Nigaud has difficulty in grasping what he has to do when documents of state are presented for his signature. His tutor patiently explains that all that is needed is for His Majesty to sign the royal name; and then by way of example takes a pen and writes out the prince's name. Thereupon Prince Nigaud likewise takes up a pen and, in the space indicated on the document, carefully copies out the example his tutor has provided.

An exasperated court might well declare that that will do well enough, and rush to get a whole backlog of documents 'signed' in the same manner, brushing aside the fact that what they are getting is the Prince's laborious imitation of his tutor's handwriting. Effective though this may be as a way of expediting affairs of state, it is clear that His Majesty has actually failed to grasp what a signature is and *pro tanto* still cannot sign his own name. However, the paradox is that by persisting in his ignorance, and encouraged therein by the court, Prince Nigaud will actually establish this misconceived autograph as the royal signature. What this shows is not the power of autocrats but the fact that the signature as such has a macrosocial aspect which cannot be ignored.

This is as true in the case of artists as of monarchs. Although it is sometimes said that signing works of art is a modern practice that has grown up because of the progressive commercialization of art, there is evidence of its acceptance in cultures far removed from any form of Western economics. Among the Maya, both painters and sculptors signed their work.[2]

The uniqueness of the signature is in some respects analogous to the uniqueness of the self-portrait. By inspecting the portrait it is impossible to tell whether it is a self-portrait or not. And, like Prince Nigaud, the painter who copied someone else's portrait of himself and thought that thereby he had painted a self-portrait, would simply bear witness to his own conceptual confusion. The distinction between portrait and self-portrait has no visible manifestation in pictorial terms. Similarly, it is impossible to tell from mere inspection of the written form whether the name was written by the person whose name it is. (There might be other clues available, but the point at issue here is whether *a form of writing* exists which proclaims authorship.

2   S.D. Houston, *Maya Glyphs* (London: British Museum, 1989), pp. 31–2.

And it does not take much reflection to realize that this is no more possible in writing than in painting.)

But again this has its paradoxical aspect, because the usual view of signatures is that if we do recognize Smith's signature as Smith's signature, it is because of the very individual way Smith *writes* it. So there seems to be a conflict here between the uniqueness and the anonymity of writing, which the signature somehow both combines and resolves.

The integrational solution to this puzzle involves pointing out that the macrosocial requirements for a signature tend to conflict with the bio-mechanical requirements. It is biomechanically impossible to produce two identically penned signatures, even with the same pen. But precisely because it is impossible from inspection of the signature to tell who wrote it, there have grown up not only practices such as the 'witnessing' of signatures (which, although perhaps an adequate social safeguard, merely multiplies the problem, since the witnesses proceed to append *their* signa-tures) but also a strong demand for consistency in the signature. Thus if I write my name in a smaller, larger or shakier hand than usual, the bank may well refuse to accept my cheque. (In a case recently reported in the press, a wealthy pop star was said to have serious difficulties with banks because he was biomechanically incapable of reproducing anything like the same signature twice. In China, this would have been no problem, because he would have used his personal seal.)

In 1930, the League of Nations encountered serious problems in estab-lishing what should count as a signature internationally.[3] These problems turned precisely on the fact that Western delegates did not regard the Oriental practice of using a seal as adequate to distinguish a genuine signature. What this highlights is a disagreement about the nature of writing. The integrational analysis would be that all parties shared the same premises about identification of the signatory, but differed macrosocially in wishing to legitimize their own traditional practices. In other words, the issue was about the activities that need to be integrated to order to effect written identification: in particular about the form of the signature and the biomechanical process of producing it. In Western eyes, the custom of using seals placed too much emphasis on replication as a guarantee of authenti-city (which one might in turn relate to Western views of 'sameness' in Oriental art), as well as leaving too many loopholes for the unauthorized use of a seal. In Eastern eyes, the insistence on the signature as a direct manual trace placed too much emphasis on the specifics of each separate signing (which one might in turn relate to Oriental perceptions of the cult of personality in Western art).

What is difficult to gainsay is that the combined macrosocial demands of recognizability and individuality favour the development of highly idio-

---

3   Béatrice Fraenkel, *La Signature. Genèse d'un signe* (Paris: Gallimard, 1992), pp. 246ff.

syncratic forms of signature, both in the East and in the West. In the East, this is seen in the deliberate diversification of signature seals, which becomes an art form *sui generis*. In the West, it results in the well-known phenomenon of the 'illegible' signature, which has become so general in Western culture that in formal documents of all kinds it is now customary to find the signatory's name typed or printed near the signature. Thus – again paradoxically – the demand that the signature be written in one's *own* hand produces a signature which in fact is not written in the signatory's *usual* hand at all, or indeed in any usual hand, and therefore cannot be deciphered by the very reader(s) for whom it is ostensibly intended.

None of this would be explicable without reference to the integrational function of the signature. Nor would the fact that the same individual may have different signatures (whether of the legible or illegible variety) which are consistently used for different purposes. Whether the name is signed 'in full', or which of several names is signed, and whether initials suffice, are matters subject to quite complex macrosocial practices in different cultures, and may depend within the culture on the social status of the signatory. Variations among these possibilities may also be used as a way of indicating an attitude on the part of the signatory towards the addressee. Thus what a signature signifies cannot be determined without reference to a number of dimensions of contextualization.

Goody understates the case when he says that in a writing culture 'the signature effectively becomes a substitute for the person'.[4] In a fully developed writing culture, the signature is actually much better than the person. For the person can hesitate, prevaricate, renege: the signature cannot. It remains valid long after the signatory is dead. What Plato saw as the great weakness of writing – its very lifelessness – becomes in the signature its greatest strength.

Of all written signs, the signature offers perhaps the richest field for research. The different types of activity for which it comes to provide an integrational nexus – its progressive extension into various domains, including commerce, art and the law, and its gradual monopoly within those domains of the role of authentication – provide the subject matter for investigations which would throw much light on many areas of social history as well as illuminating numerous points of interest for the semiologist.[5]

---

4 J. Goody, *The Logic of Writing and the Organization of Society* (Cambridge: Cambridge University Press, 1986), p. 152.
5 Fraenkel, *La Signature*, provides an admirable pioneering study for the Western tradition. It would be of great value to have parallel studies for other parts of the world, as well as more detailed studies of signing practices in specific socio-cultural domains.

Chapter 12

Sign and signification

According to traditional theories of glottic writing, the written sign takes its signification from the spoken sign that it represents. Thus the written word *daffodil* is assumed to have a meaning which answers exactly to – and is determined by – the meaning of the corresponding word in spoken English.

This is all in accordance with the traditional (Aristotelian) theory of the written sign as metasign, and may seem to be plain common sense to a generation brought up to 'read for meaning', i.e. to believe that reading is a matter of extracting the verbal meanings from marks displayed on a page.

From an integrational point of view, however, one problem with this assumption is that it leaves no room for the possibility that the written form itself contributes anything to what the written sign signifies. And this, as the case of the signature amply demonstrates, cannot be so. Furthermore, it leaves a theoretical blank in those areas of writing where there is in any case no corresponding spoken word to provide a putative meaning for the written form.

The cases discussed below situate these problems of signification in an integrational framework.

1 Plate 10 provides an example of a use of writing which is common enough in Britain today, although perhaps occasionally perplexing to some foreign visitors. It involves the deliberate choice of unusual or exotic letter forms.

For the integrationist, what this signifies goes beyond the mere identification of the word *antiques*. It presupposes a reading competence in which, at the very least, the choice of Gothic lettering is recognized as part of the written message; and, specifically, as having been chosen in order to evoke associations with bygone times. (Whether it actually does this is another question, and what the basis for such associations might be another question again. Nevertheless, 𝔄𝔫𝔱𝔦𝔮𝔲𝔢𝔰 signifies something other than, say, 𝖠𝗇𝗍𝗂𝗊𝗎𝖾𝗌.)

Modern advertising has seen the invention of letter forms which have no other function than to signify in this mode. A conspicuous example (Plate 11) is the use of pseudo-Oriental letter forms for writing English.

One way of dealing with such cases is to dismiss the choice of letter forms as 'decorative' or 'stylistic'. But this is semiologically naive for a number of reasons; not least because it assumes that in the first place a word was chosen and only *then* did the question arise of how to 'write' it. From an integrational point of view, this simply does not correspond to anyone's experience of modern graphic design, either as writer or as reader.

2 In typography, there is a practice sometimes known as 'greeking'. This involves the use of characters 'to show what the real copy will look like when pasted into place or to give the illusion of copy in an illustration where real copy is not needed'.[1]

Quto avoi bxyo mnstr laeyo aoiou dxpo. Bzny cmbent dtnsti pxrnxo. Dxpo quto avoi bxyo mnstr laeyo aoiou. Pxrnxo bzny cmbent dtnsti. Aoiou dxpo quto avoi bxyo mnstr laeyo. Dtnsti pxrnxo cmbent. Laeyo aoiou dxpo quto avoi bxyo mnstr. Bzny cmbent dtnsti pxrnxo. Mnstr laeyo aoiou dxpo quto auoi bxyo. Pxrnxo bzny cmbnet dtnsti. Bxyo mnstr laeyo aoiou dxpo quto auoi. Stnsti pxrnxo bzny cmbent. Avoi bxno mnstr laeyo aoio dxpo quto. Dmbent dtnsti pxrnxo bzny. Quto avoi bxyo mnstr laeyo aoiou dxpo. Bzny cmbent dtnsti pxrnxo. Dxpo quto laeyo

From a traditional point of view, this is presumably not writing at all; or at best pseudo-writing. For there are no spoken words to supply the meanings for such graphic forms as *quto, avoi*, etc. And since these graphic forms are therefore meaningless, they cannot be read, and it follows that the text cannot 'really' be writing.

From an integrational point of view, such an analysis simply confirms the poverty of traditional accounts of writing. The fact is that the rationale of greeking is perfectly clear when we put it in its proper context: the printed forms have their signification, but it is a signification not related to speech, even indirectly.

Greeking is an interesting practice because, in integrational terms, it illustrates the limiting case where the function of the written sign coincides with the visual processing of the written forms. To put it another way, processing and interpretation are one; or again, the sole interpretation required is that yielded by processing.

3 *Pseudo-writing* is a term sometimes given by anthropologists to a practice institutionalized in certain cultures. It involves the production by a shaman, usually in a trance, of graphic texts which are then interpreted as predictions.

---

1 P.B. Mintz, *Dictionary of Graphic Art Terms* (New York: Van Nostrand Reinhold, 1981), p. 103.

A recent case in which pseudo-writing may have played a part in the creation of a 'genuine' writing system is that of Shong Lue Yang (1929–71), inventor of the Hmong alphabet.[2] In the community from which he came, pseudo-writing is practised by recognized fortune-tellers (*shau*). When consulted about the future, the *shau* goes into a trance and produces lines of marks on paper (Plate 12). On coming out of the trance, the *shau* reads these marks and gives a prediction.

No one except the *shau* can read the text thus produced. Furthermore, the *shau* cannot read it after a few days have elapsed, nor give the interpretation of any sequence of marks taken at random, nor take down a text from dictation. In short, the *shau* cannot 'read' or 'write' in the usual Western sense.

How such a practice develops in an otherwise illiterate community remains unexplained by Western theories of writing.

The phenomenon described above is open to an integrational analysis which does not involve postulating that the *shau* is a fake, or that the form of writing produced is devoid of signification.

There are good grounds for supposing (see paragraph 4 below) that the biomechanical act of inscription may itself be instrumental as a mnemonic device. (A common experience is that writing down a name or number is itself sufficient to aid recall, without subsequent recourse to the written text itself.) If it is assumed that the *shau* is not engaged in a confidence trick, we are led to suppose that a vision of the future induced in trance is mentally 'recorded' by means of the motoric processes involved in inscription. In other words, the *shau* has developed a way of integrating trance experiences with the 'normal' world, by means of a biomechanical programme that links both. After the trance, inspection of the marks facilitates a reconstruction of the vision that occasioned their inscription.

4   The term *pseudo-writing*, as it happens, might also be applied to a graphic ability shown by some children and first demonstrated in an experiment conducted by Luria. This showed that with the help of paper and pencil it was possible for children who could not yet read or write in the traditional sense to make marks which enabled them later to recall and distinguish orally dictated sentences.

Luria identifies various stages in the development of 'scribbling' as the child's aid to oral recall. In the first stage, the scribbling is undifferentiated and does not appear to have any mnemonic function. In the second stage, although still apparently undifferentiated – at least, to an adult eye – the scribbles somehow enable the child to identify and distinguish between dictated items.

2   W.A. Smalley, C.K. Vang and G.Y. Yang, *Mother of Writing. The Origin and Development of a Hmong Messianic Script* (Chicago: University of Chicago Press, 1990), pp. 97ff.

We checked this and indeed discovered that these scribblings actually were more than just simple scrawls, that they were in some sense real writing. The child would read a sentence, pointing to quite specific scrawls, and was able to show without error and many times in succession which scribble signified which of the dictated sentences. Writing was still undifferentiated in its outward appearance, but the child's relationship to it had completely changed: from a self-contained motor activity, it had been transformed into a memory-helping sign.[3]

What is happening here, in integrational terms, is that the 'scribbled' sign has acquired a signification. For biomechanical reasons yet unknown, the mark the child makes fulfils an integrational function in the sequence of activities that links the original dictation (an auditory experience) with the eventual re-identification of the items dictated.

5 Yet another form of 'pseudo-writing' is exemplified by a recent American advertisement introducing a new ice-cream. The poster depicts an ice-cream carton on which appears the following text:

Häagen-Dazs

EXTRÄAS

The written form *exträas* belongs to no known language and *Häagen-Dazs* is an invented brand name. Nevertheless, the former acquires an implication of glottic function from its juxtaposition with the latter, and both rely on the reader's vague recognition of the spelling as 'Scandinavian'. Given the reader's acquaintance with the brand name *Häagen-Dazs*, the orthographic similarity between the form *exträas* and the English word *extra* is presumably sufficient to suggest a signification which will serve the purpose of the advertiser's message.

6 The visual resemblance between graphic forms can be exploited to produce signs of which the interpretation presupposes the reader's acquaintance with that resemblance and with the associations thereby evoked. The production of such a sign can even alert readers to a resemblance of which they were not previously aware.

For example, the visual resemblance between a capital letter **E** and a swastika may not, at first sight, be apparent. But anyone familiar with recent French elections will recall how the name of a prominent politician of the far right, which happened to include the letter **E**, frequently appeared in

---

3 A.R. Luria, 'The development of writing in the child', in M. Cole (ed.), *The Selected Writings of A.R. Luria* (White Plains, N.Y.: Sharpe, 1978), p. 159.

graffiti in a form in which the **E** had somehow been transformed into a shape curiously resembling a swastika. A visual association of this nature would be quite meaningless outside the particular communicational context which gave birth to it.

Similarly, although the resemblance between the letter **s** and the dollar sign is more obvious, it requires a combination of circumstances to give signification to the newspaper headline which announced revelations concerning a former mayor's alleged mismanagement of campaign funds as:

Flynn's fia$co

*   *   *

The different types of case mentioned above are connected. They illustrate various facets of what is, from an integrational point of view, a single semiological principle: that the signification of a sign has no other source than the contextualized complex of activities which it integrates. The integration involved does not necessarily require the use of a traditional writing system. On the contrary, a traditional writing system simply represents the macrosocial systematization of semiological skills which are far more basic.

Part III

Topics in the theory of writing systems

Chapter 13

Writing, script and chart

From an integrational point of view, there is no reason to restrict the phenomenon of writing to the use of traditionally established alphabets, syllabaries, etc. In any case, a traditionally established set of graphic units does not necessarily have to be used in traditionally established ways (as the development of cryptography demonstrates). Even when the traditional characters are used in writing, the semiology of the written message will depend on the communicational context and the activities thus integrated.

For many theorists, however, writing is nothing other than the use of some set of traditional characters, and consequently their account of the forms that writing may take is limited to a survey of such cases.

For the semiologist, this narrow perspective has no justification, because any information recorded by traditional means can in principle also be recorded without using a script at all.

For instance, in modern Western culture telephone numbers are commonly identified by sequences of Arabic numerals: for example, 617–353–7275. Anyone wishing to record this information can do so by writing down this set of digits. Let us call this text 1 (T1).

Anyone who wished to record this information, but not in a form which would reveal the number to all and sundry, could disguise it by translating it into a sequence of alphabetic letters, e.g. FAG CEC GBGE. Let us call this text 2 (T2).

In both forms, T1 and T2, traditional characters are used, and the cryptogram in the second case is derived by a simple process of matching the characters of one inventory with the characters of another.

The same information could be recorded, however, in a quite different form; for instance, by taking a ten-by-ten grid of squared paper, and filling in one square in each column. Let us call this text 3 (T3: Fig. 13.1).

In T3, each row of the grid is understood as 'representing' one of the ten digits.

Here we are dealing with a mode of communication which might, perhaps, be called 'writing' but to do so would blur an important semiological difference, even though the information recorded in T3 is the same

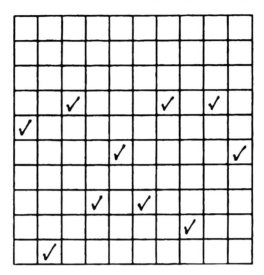

Figure 13.1

as in T1 and T2. The difference has nothing to do with whether the message in question is verbal or non-verbal: a larger and longer grid of squared paper, containing twenty-six rows and many more columns, would make it possible in principle to record the complete works of Shakespeare.

Thus it is important to be clear about why T3, from an integrationist's point of view, falls into a different graphic category from T1 or T2; and in particular to be clear that the reason is not simple deference to traditional usage of the term *writing*. On the contrary, to deny T3 the status of writing simply on the ground that it dispenses with the use of traditional written characters would be a move with no theoretical justification at all. (It could equally well be argued that the system used in T3 *is* a script (albeit an unconventional one), precisely on the ground that its capacity for recording information is in no way inferior to that of any 'normal' script.)

The temptation to dismiss this and related issues by the arbitrary adoption of definitions of terms is to be resisted. If a term such as *script* is to be used as a theoretical term, its use needs a theoretical rationale, and this rationale must come from the semiological framework adopted in one's analysis.

Looking at the question from an integrational point of view, there are clearly important features of the activities which need to be integrated in order to form, process and interpret T3, which set it apart from T1 and T2. These differences hinge on the fact that the characters in T1 and T2 have been replaced by the assignment of places in a two-dimensional array.

When I write down 617–353–7275 or FAG CEC GBGE, there is no analogue whatsoever to the activity of locating the correct squares in each column of the grid of T3. Filling in the grid correctly requires the exercise of spatial skills and associated mapping procedures which are not demanded at all in setting down a string of characters. Setting down a string of characters requires mastery of the formative features of a whole set of differentiated marks; but the 'mark' used to fill in a square is always the same, or else – which amounts to the same thing – it does not matter what the 'mark' is provided it unambiguously identifies one particular square. (From an integrational point of view, it is a token: Ch. 10.) If in scanning a grid message I 'misread' the level of the mark in the first column, I may consequentially and systematically misread all the rest. Whereas if I misread the initial digit 6 as 5, there is no possibility of a consequential misreading of 617–353–7275 as 506–242–6164.

Differences of this order are intuitively obvious and presumably have a biomechanical basis, although exactly how the differences involved translate into motor or neurological programmes it is not for the semiologist to say. Nor does it greatly matter what terminology the semiologist employs in order to give theoretical recognition to the distinction. However, the traditional term *script* corresponds well enough to the typical range of forming and processing activities involved in dealing with letters, numerals, syllabaries, etc. These activities are based on the recognition and relative sequencing of the members of an inventory of characters, differentiated not by their absolute locations in a given graphic space but by their form. On this basis, therefore, it is proposed here to distinguish between graphic communi-cation which uses a script and graphic communication which does not.

A system which makes semiological use of absolute locations in a given graphic space, as in the case of T3, will here be referred to as a *chart*.

What is being claimed, therefore, is that using a script as a technique of communication is basically different – in the forming, processing and interpretation required – from using a chart.[1]

There will, however, be 'mixed' systems which combine both script and chart. For instance, it would be possible – although quite redundant – to fill in the appropriate squares of T3 with the corresponding Arabic numerals, thus recording the telephone number simultaneously in script and chart form.

Redundancy of this kind is actually attested in the case of labels on supermarket merchandise, where the same information is recorded both in the form of a thirteen-digit figure and in the form of a so-called 'bar code'

---

1 It may perhaps be objected that this claim rests on the adoption of stipulative definitions of the terms *script* and *chart*, and so incurs the same strictures as were levelled above against resolving issues by the adoption of definitions. Such an objection, however, misses the point. The distinction between *script* and *chart* is theoretically motivated, whether we decide to use those particular terms or any others. Similarly, even if it were decided to extend the term *writing* to include the uses of charts, it would then become necessary to distinguish between *script-writing* and *chart-writing* on the same basis.

Figure 13.2 Script and chart combined.

(Fig 13.2). In the bar code, the graphic space is subdivided into sections, each of which is seven units wide, and each unit of which is either 'dark' or 'light'. The visual contrast between the numeral and the bar code juxtaposed to it illustrates in a very striking way the integrationist's distinction between script and chart. The difference between the two corresponds, moreover, to a very clear difference between the activities integrated, that is, between scanning by the human eye and scanning by a laser pencil.

More interesting from a semiological point of view are those mixed systems which employ features of both script and chart, but in such a way as to separate out different kinds of information in the message.

Thus, for instance, modern musical notation which uses a display of notes on a stave is a typical 'mixed system' of this kind: the notes are different from one another in shape (♪♫ etc.) and their sequence relative to one another is significant, but the location of each in the graphic space provided by the five-line stave, functioning as a chart, is also essential to the musical message (Ch. 21). In order to 'read' music, we have to deploy two different processing techniques simultaneously.[2]

2   It seems intuitively obvious that the chart interpretation is a harder job than the script interpretation: i.e. the main difficulty in sight-reading a musical score is not in identifying the duration of the notes or their sequence but in locating their pitch.

Chapter 14

Scripts and levels

The integrational potential of a writing system is manifestly dependent on the macrosocial distribution of knowledge relevant to its use, including linguistic knowledge. A broad distinction may be drawn here between *glottic* and *non-glottic writing* depending on whether the formation and interpretation of texts presupposes knowledge of a particular language (e.g. English, Latin, Urdu).

The theory of glottic scripts commonly adopted by linguists distinguishes different kinds of writing system according to which units in the spoken language appear to have been selected as the basic units for representation in writing. The correspondence between writing and speech established in this way is sometimes referred to as the 'level' of the script.[1]

The 'levels' approach leads to a typology of the kind proposed by Saussure (described above in Ch. 3), which distinguished between scripts representing words (termed 'ideographic' scripts by Saussure), scripts representing syllables and scripts representing individual sounds in the speech chain. The latter two are subsumed under the heading of 'phonetic' or 'phonological' scripts. (Saussure uses both the term *phonétique* and the term *phonologique*, apparently without distinguishing between the two.)

Variants of this typology draw finer distinctions, such as between 'word writing' and 'morpheme writing', or between 'phonetic writing' and 'phonemic writing'. Although the terminology varies, most linguists since Saussure have followed his major division into two levels, the *fundamentum divisionis* being whether or not the lowest-level units represented in a script are independently meaningful in the spoken language. Haas calls these two levels 'pleremic' and 'cenemic'.[2] Sampson calls them 'logographic' and 'phonographic'.[3]

Schemes of this kind, clearly, treat writing basically as a mirror of speech,

---

1 F. Coulmas, *Writing Systems of the World* (Oxford: Blackwell, 1989), pp. 49–50.
2 W. Haas, 'Determining the level of a script', in F. Coulmas and K. Ehlich (eds), *Writing in Focus* (Berlin: Mouton, 1983), pp. 15–29.
3 G. Sampson, *Writing Systems* (London: Hutchinson, 1985), p. 32.

and writing systems as differing typologically one from another principally in the levels of speech organization they reflect. This much is acknowledged by Sampson, who relates the distinction between logographic and phono-graphic systems to the 'double articulation'[4] of speech into meaningful (or 'first-articulation') units and meaningless (or 'second-articulation') units. It is likewise implied by the terms 'pleremic' (i.e. 'full') and 'cenemic' (i.e. 'empty').

One initial oddity about this typology is worth noting, since it has theoretical implications. The double articulation of speech is simultaneous: that is, the choice is not between having a spoken language which has *either* a first articulation *or else* a second articulation; nor vice versa. Furthermore, and more importantly, the two articulations of speech are not independent, inasmuch as no spoken language in everyday use has *only* a first articulation, or *only* a second articulation (the latter being an impossibility by definition).

Now in theory there is no reason why a glottic writing system should not also have a doubly articulated structure in the same way; and there is a simple and plausible case for saying that many writing systems in fact do. (The only requirement is that second-articulation graphic units should be organized into first-articulation complexes, for instance by word-dividers or other devices.) This suggests that a more rational typology – from the viewpoint of these theorists – would have been to make the *fundamentum divisionis* the question of whether or not a glottic script has double articulation.

According to Elmar Holenstein,[5] what 'deterred leading phonologists from describing writing analogously to speech as a doubly articulated system' was not the lack of structural isomorphism or local imperfections but 'the absence of a functional isomorphism'. That is to say, whereas letters were assumed to represent phonemes, phonemes represented nothing. If this explanation is correct, it is striking testimony to the way in which the initial assumption made by Saussure paralysed the analysis of writing systems for a generation or more. It is rather like refusing to recognize the correspondence between an object and its image in the mirror, not because the image is only partial or distorted but on the curious ground that whereas the image functions as a reflection of the object, the object does not function as a reflection of anything.

What lies behind the linguists' binary division of levels, one suspects, is something else: their long preoccupation with sound systems, the analysis of which has been the basis of their discipline since the early nineteenth

---

4   *Double articulation* is defined by linguists as follows: 'At one level, language is analysed into combinations of meaningful units (such as words and sentences); at the other level, it is analysed as a sequence of phonological segments which lack meaning.' (D. Crystal, *An Encyclopedic Dictionary of Language and Languages* (Oxford: Blackwell, 1992), p. 110).

5   E. Holenstein, 'Double articulation in writing', in F. Coulmas and K. Ehlich (eds), *Writing in Focus* (Berlin: Mouton, 1983), pp. 47–8.

century. Once language is equated with speech, a pleremic script is relatively uninteresting because it yields no information about how the language studied is – or might have been – pronounced. In other words, the typology of levels adopted is tacitly based not on the distinction 'meaningful' versus 'meaningless', as is claimed, but rather on the distinction 'phonetically informative' versus 'phonetically uninformative'.

However, there is a more important question to be addressed in the present context: how satisfactory is such a typology from a semiological point of view?

The basis of the typology is ostensibly semiological (in that it takes what is signified as the main criterion for classifying a writing system) but it is arbitrary in various respects. Why a simple matching between characters and units in the spoken language should be taken as *ipso facto* determining the typological classification of a writing system is far from clear. Furthermore, the typology presupposes that a clear answer can be given to the question of what a given written character 'represents', and leaves us in doubt about how to proceed when this is uncertain.

For instance, as Haas points out, linguistic units often belong to more than one level. In *a book* the first letter represents a unit which, in spoken English, is simultaneously a phoneme, a syllable, a morpheme and a word. Does this mean that English is written in a mixed system, i.e. is partly 'pleremic'? Coulmas, following Haas, seeks to avoid this conclusion by claiming that we must distinguish between (i) the level of 'the basic operational unit of a system' and (ii) information that may be conveyed, either accidentally or deliberately, about units at other levels. Because the 'rules' by which this form of the English indefinite article is assigned the written symbol *a* are (so it is claimed) 'phoneme–grapheme correspondence rules', we can treat as accidental the fact that the form in question also happens to be meaningful.

The reasoning deployed to reach this solution of the problem is baffling. It certainly belies any notion that what is being applied here is a semiological classification. The 'rules' conjured up in support of the argument are simply theoretical constructs devised by the analyst: in other words, it is the analyst who is making the 'assignment' of letters to sounds, not the users of the writing system. The fact that any reader with a minimal degree of literacy in English, on seeing the single letter *a* standing in isolation before *book*, immediately knows that this signifies the indefinite article, *regardless of how it might be pronounced in reading aloud*, counts for nothing. And the fact that the spelling *a* is in any case phonemically ambiguous seems to have dropped out of sight altogether.

In short, from an integrational point of view, this is bogus semiology.

Unfortunately, it is also disingenuous linguistics from any point of view. For what is going on in the 'analysis' of the writing system is actually an elaborate exercise in projecting the phonology of English on to the traditional orthography of English. And here we come to more fundamental criticisms of the 'levels' approach.

In order to establish the 'correspondences' between written and spoken units for a language such as English, the analyst apparently starts from the pronunciations of isolated words (as registered e.g. in an orthoepic diction-ary) and breaks them down segmentally, relying on tacit appeals to analogy whenever the correspondence is problematic. (Thus in order to make *cough* correspond to /kof/ in the way that *bat* corresponds to /bat/ there needs to be some manipulation of the segmentation procedure: i.e. strictly, the only plausible segmentation of *cough* yields five graphic units, but to recognize five phonemes here, or the presence of 'dummy' letters, would be as unacceptable to these analysts as to leave *cough* as a single orthographic unit.) The theoretical motivation for this sleight of hand is readily under-standable: what is objectionable is that the resultant equivalences are then passed off as 'rules' which structure the whole writing system *at the phoneme level.* In other words, the real comparison is being tacitly conducted all the time at the word level (i.e. the 'pleremic' level); but the results are being offered as discoveries about how phonemes are represented (i.e. at the 'cenemic' level). Which begs the question of whether phonemes are being represented in the first place.

That is not all. There is a further layer of doublethink. It can be illustrated by reference to supposedly unproblematic equivalences of the type

bat : /bat/

where the traditional orthography of the English word matches exactly its phonemic transcription. This correspondence notwithstanding, the claim that the alphabetic letters of *bat* represent phonemes of English (as distinct from sounds) stands history on its head: for phonemes themselves are in the first instance theoretical idealizations extrapolated from letters of the alphabet.

So to anyone acquainted with the development of modern phonology it hardly comes as a surprise that the phonemic equivalent of *bat* turns out to be /bat/. Phonemic transcription uses an alphabetically based writing system, and always has done. When *bat* is said to represent /bat/, the claim is all the more likely to go unchallenged in that the correspondence appears to be *visible* on the printed page for all to see. We perhaps need to remind ourselves that /bat/ itself is a written form no less than *bat*, and the 'visible' equivalence between the two is the product of the close historical rela-tionship between two glottic forms of writing. One of these is traditional and the other invented by modern phonologists; but the second is derived from the first.

Corresponding both to *bat* and to /bat/, it may be urged, we find the same spoken English word; but that is a rather different and perhaps less controversial proposition than the claim that the alphabetic letters of *bat* represent exactly the same set of abstract entities as the alphabetic letters of /bat/. The phonologist's form /bat/ presumably does represent a sequence of English phonemes (however these entities are defined) because it was designed to do just that; but whether the traditional spelling *bat* does likewise or ever did is another matter.

From an integrational point of view, what the crude typology of levels misses altogether is the possibility that there may be more than one semiologically relevant structural patterning in a script. That this is so in the case of English is so obvious that it is difficult to regard any attempt to prove that English writing is purely cenemic as more than a theoretically misguided exercise in ingenuity. In countless cases, English traditional spelling disambiguates words that are phonologically indistinguishable. If English writing were purely cenemic, these random variations of spelling would have to be reckoned a blemish or defect in the system. But to regard them thus would be not merely perverse: it would be, semiologically, nonsensical. The whole point of distinguishing homonyms orthographically is that they function differently as signs.

There is a more general question involved, which goes much further than any specific features of written English. What the typology of levels fails to capture is the distinction between a script and a notation (see Ch. 15). In fact, it conflates the two.

This conflation can be traced to the basic assumption underlying the typology: that writing exists solely to represent speech. The assumption, as already noted in Chapter 3, is explicitly stated by Saussure. For theorists who make that assumption, whether they do so explicitly or not, the problem is how then to explain away the fact that in so many instances writing appears actually to *mis*represent speech. In the *Cours de linguistique générale*, two whole sections of Chapter VI of the Introduction are devoted to the subject of the 'discrepancy' (*désaccord*) between writing and pronunciation. The discussion of writing in the *Cours* goes so far as to claim that 'writing obscures our view of the language'[6] and to speak of *la tyrannie de la lettre*.[7] This, according to Saussure, is one of the consequences of literacy which handicaps the linguist's objective investigation of speech:

> the written word is so intimately connected with the spoken word it represents that it manages to usurp the principal role. As much or even more importance is given to this representation of the vocal sign as to the vocal sign itself. It is rather as if people believed that in order to find out what a person looks like it is better to study his photograph than his face.[8]

What, then, is the source of those discrepancies between scripts and their

6   F. de Saussure, *Cours de linguistique générale*, 2nd edn (Paris: Payot, 1922), p. 51.
7   *Ibid.*, p. 53.
8   *Ibid.*, p. 45.

(alleged) representational functions? Saussure says there are many factors involved, but mentions only the three he considers most important.

1 The most general is that spoken language constantly tends to change, whereas writing tends to remain static (*immobile*). Example: the modern French spelling of the word for 'king' (*roi*) reflects its thirteenth-century pronunciation.

As an explanation, this is curious on several counts. Its explanatory force is obscure, since no cause has been identified. The allegedly static character of the written form is merely a retrospective description of the fact that a modern spelling (*roi*) corresponds exactly to a medieval spelling (*roi*). The history of French spelling offers many similar examples. But to conclude from such cases that writing is static already presupposes that the same principles of phonetic representation apply to both the earlier and the later forms; in other words, that twentieth-century orthography is to be assessed on the same basis as the orthography of the medieval scribe.

But in that case the explanation of the phenomenon damages the original thesis; for it emerges that alphabetic writing, whatever else it may be, cannot be purely and simply phonetic writing. Otherwise, the spelling *roi* would have changed, unless different principles of representation apply at different times.

There is a complementary puzzle. It is hard to see why French writers today should not adopt the spelling *rwa*, or any other which they feel better represents the pronunciation of the word, *if indeed that is their view of the function of orthography*. And if it is, then to attribute to them a preference for the orthography of the thirteenth century would be, to say the least, odd.

It is difficult here to exculpate Saussure from the charge he is elsewhere keen to press against other theorists; namely, a confusion of synchronic and diachronic perspectives. For if there are indeed 'discrepancies' between spelling and pronunciation, these can only be synchronic discrepancies, and as such call for synchronic explanations. Explaining the modern spelling by reference to the medieval pronunciation is thus itself problematic: the notion of a 'diachronic spelling' makes no sense.[9]

2 The second factor Saussure identifies is that writing systems are often 'borrowed' and do not fit the language of the borrowers.

---

9 Saussure is by no means the only linguist open to criticism on this score. The muddle continues today. Sampson, for example, says of French spelling that certain words 'were at one time invariably pronounced with the final consonants (as they are still written in standard French orthography)' (*Writing Systems*, p. 134). This seems to imply that French as currently written represents French pronunciations, but some of them happen to be the pronunciations of centuries past. The same linguist also speaks of the way in which current English orthography represents 'obsolete surface pronunciations' (*Ibid.*, p. 140). How modern English spelling, as a synchronic system, can simultaneously represent sounds of quite different diachronic status remains a mystery that is never elucidated.

It often happens that the resources of the graphic system are poorly adapted to its new function, and it is necessary to have recourse to various expedients. Two letters, for example, will be used to designate a single sound.[10]

Saussure cites the example of the German voiceless dental fricative, which was written *th* because the Latin alphabet had no corresponding letter.

Again, paradoxically, Saussure's explanation undermines his main thesis. Adopting *th* to represent a voiceless dental fricative makes little sense if it is true that each letter has its own phonetic value, since *th* would in that case represent something different, i.e. a voiceless dental stop followed by an aspirate. Saussure notes that King Chilperic had tried to introduce a special alphabetic sign for the voiceless dental fricative, but without success. The King's failure is puzzling if Saussure's view of alphabetic writing is correct; for that is precisely the solution Saussure's theory would predict.

3 The third factor Saussure appeals to is etymology.

> Etymological preoccupations also intrude. They were particularly notice-able at certain periods, such as the Renaissance. It is not infrequently the case that a spelling is introduced through mistaken etymologising: *d* was thus introduced in the French word *poids* ('weight'), as if it came from Latin *pondus*, when in fact it comes from *pensum*. But it makes little difference whether the etymology is correct or not. It is the principle of etymological spelling itself which is mistaken.[11]

Once more the explanation Saussure offers sabotages his own theory of alphabetic writing; but in this instance the argument is blatantly question-begging. For it is little short of absurd for a twentieth-century theorist to claim to be able to tell Renaissance writers that they were wrong in the orthographic principles they adopted; particularly when this accusation is brought in order to support a thesis which is itself open to serious doubt.

Nothing reveals more clearly than the various explanations Saussure puts forward that the very notion of 'discrepancy' between speech and writing is itself the product of a prescriptivist attitude towards the written language; and specifically of the prescriptivist thesis that spelling 'ought' to be determined by pronunciation.

From an integrational point of view, no serious semiology of writing can be established on prescriptivist foundations of this kind.

10 *Cours*, p. 49.
11 *Ibid.*, p. 50.

Chapter 15

Scripts and notations

An integrational theory of writing systems draws a distinction between scripts and the notations on which they are based. The reason for this distinction is that it corresponds to the integration of typically different activities in the two cases.

Failure to acknowledge such a distinction is one of the omissions which vitiates any theory of levels of the kind discussed in Chapter 14. But the distinction itself is not obscure: on the contrary, it is apparent to relatively unsophisticated lay observation. Any English student learning French soon comes to realize that the same sequence of alphabetic letters *c-h-a-i-r* spells one word in English, but a quite different word with a quite different meaning in French. The words are different, but the letters are not. In semiological terms, therefore, the written sign cannot be identified simply with the sequence of letters.

The implications of this simple distinction for a theory of writing systems are considerable.

The alphabet is not, as Saussure mistakenly thought, a writing system functioning at one particular level of (mis)representation (i.e. the phonetic level). More importantly, the alphabet is not a writing system at all. It is a notation.

A notation may, in principle, serve to articulate any number of different writing systems.

Both glottic and non-glottic writing systems may be based on notations. A familiar example of a non-glottic writing system which is notationally based is that of elementary arithmetic, based on the so-called Arabic numerals. This notation is used for many different writing systems. Its characters do not have fixed quantitative values except within the scope of a particular writing system. It would be naive to suppose that the figure 5, for instance, is the visual symbol for a quantitative constant that it 'represents' in all arithmetic expressions. For the figure 5 remains itself even when it has no arithmetic value at all; as when, for instance, it functions as part of a telephone number or post code. Whatever value the figure 5 has (and this will vary according to context), it remains recognizable as a member of the series of characters belonging to the notation we call 'Arabic numerals'.

Similarly, we may recognize the letters *c-h-a-i-r* even when they occur in a text we do not understand (for instance, because the text happens to be written in French and we do not read French). But it would be rash to jump to the conclusion that this was a French text that included English words.

Integrationally, the relationship between notation and script may be articulated in a number of ways, but it will always involve a significant difference in the activities integrated. A copyist or typist may well be able to transcribe a text in an unfamiliar language. Such an enterprise does not require 'reading' in the everyday sense of that word; but it involves both visual processing and interpretation (as those terms were defined in Chapter 9). What is happening in such a case is that the text is being processed and interpreted on the basis of its notation. Understanding the writing system is actually irrelevant to the activities thus integrated. (It may even be a hindrance.)

From an integrational point of view, a notation is not simply a writing system minus the values attached to the written forms. It will have its own structure, which is not derived from the script or scripts which it serves to implement. This independence may initially seem surprising; but it has analogues in other forms of communication (see Appendix A).

For instance, if we wish to write the number 'thirteen' in Arabic numerals, we have a choice between various systems. Depending on the system chosen, the result might be *13*, or *1101*, or *111*, or *31*, or *23*, or *21*, or *11*. All the systems thus exemplified utilize the same notation, but make different selections from the resources it offers.

This brings into focus an important fact that cannot be accommodated at all in a Saussurean theory of scripts: *there may be more than one structural principle at work in the articulation of a single expression.* Let us take, for example, the expression of 'thirteen' in the binary system: *1101*. Here the syntagmatic organization and the numerical values are supplied by the binary system; but the form of the two figures and their relative priority come from the notation itself and not from the binary system (which in principle could employ ∞ and §, or ¶ and •, or any two symbols whatsoever, provided the two were consistently differentiated).

Similarly, if we compare the expressions *13* and *31*, we see that the individual characters are the same but their syntagmatic arrangement differs. This difference has nothing to do with the notation, but has to be referred to the fact that the denary system and the quaternary system have different syntagmatic structures.

The number 'thirteen' can also be expressed in Roman letters. For arithmetic purposes, Roman notation employs the seven letters *I, V, X, L, C, D* and *M*. As far as their forms are concerned, these are letters of the alphabet. But their order is not that of the Latin alphabet. Here it is the arithmetic writing system which imposes another order, on the basis of the values 'one', 'five', 'ten', 'fifty', 'hundred', 'five hundred' and 'thousand'.

The result is that 'thirteen' is written *XIII*. Again, the syntagmatic structure is not determined by the notation.

Alphabetical order, on the other hand, which is widely used for listing purposes in cultures employing alphabetic writing, often has nothing to do with the writing system. Thus the alphabetical order in Latin, French and English dictionaries is quite independent of the systems of writing employed in writing the Latin, French and English texts of those dictionaries. In each case it is a feature of notation.

That notations can develop independently of the writing systems with which they are associated is clearly shown by the case of the runic alphabet, or *futhark*, which is an offshoot from the same branch that produced the Greek and Roman alphabets. However, the runic 'alphabetical order' is quite different (Fig. 15.1), and the set of characters is internally divided into three sections or 'families' of eight characters each – a feature that has no analogue in any other form of alphabetic writing. That this is a genuine feature of the notation as such is shown by (a) the fact that it has no basis in the phonetic values assigned to the runes in any of the known languages they were used to write, and (b) the fact that this division was used as a point of reference for constructing alternative forms of the runes themselves. (Thus, for example, the second rune in the first division could be noted by a vertical line having two branches on one side and a single branch on the opposite side, corresponding to its order in the 'family' and the order of the 'family' in the *futhark* respectively.[1]) A derived secondary system of this

Figure 15.1 Runic alphabet.

1 E.H. Antonsen, 'The runes: the earliest Germanic writing system', in W.M. Senner (ed.), *The Origins of Writing* (Lincoln and London: University of Nebraska Press, 1989), p. 142.

kind constitutes a metanotation, comparable to the braille alphabet and the Morse code.

Far more complex relations between notation and writing systems are to be found (Plate 13).

Elements of notation typically have designations of their own, and these can be incorporated into messages articulated by the writing system to which they belong. Thus in

PLEN*T*PAK

the letter *T* has to be 'read' as the syllable *tee* in order to make up the word *plenty*. That it is not to be read as the 'ordinary' letter *T* is indicated by its differentiation in size and colour from the accompanying letter forms. The message would be incomprehensible if readers could not recognize the difference between the two levels of structuring. An even more complex application of the same principle is to be found in runic writing, where the rune names are also meaningful words. Thus it becomes possible to use a single rune as an abbreviation for a whole word in a text otherwise 'spelt out' in full.[2]

None of these aspects of writing can be handled satisfactorily by a semiological theory which fails to distinguish notations from writing systems.

2   R.I. Page, *Runes* (London: British Museum, 1987), p. 16.

Chapter 16

Script and structure

From an integrational point of view, any structure is a pattern of features which can, in the right context, be of communicational relevance and thus have a communicational function. Whether it does in practice have such a function is another matter; that is, whether it does actually contribute to the formation and interpretation of signs.

Scripts invariably confer additional structuring on the notations they utilize. In this respect, the script may be considered as consisting of a notation plus a set of procedures for deploying it. In principle there is no reason why two or more scripts should not share the same notation, but deploy that notation in accordance with different procedures. That is why it is essential to distinguish between structuring which derives from the notation and structuring which derives from the script.

Failure to distinguish between script and notation leads directly to implausible and unobservant analyses of scripts, all the more so when this failure is combined with slavish adherence to a theory of levels.

For example, there is a pattern in contemporary English linking written words which end in -gh to spoken words which end in a voiceless labio-dental fricative consonant:

cough, rough, tough, enough, etc.

Those analysts who treat English writing as cenemic seize upon this 'evidence' to claim that there exists in English spelling a digraph *gh* with a specific phonetic value.

They are not so keen to recognize the existence of this digraph in words like *eight*. Does it there represent a silent variant of the fricative? Or is *ght* a trigraph representing the final dental stop? Or is *eigh* a tetragraph representing the diphthong of the word *eight*? We are rarely told, because it would be embarrassing to pursue the segmentation procedure doggedly that far. But if need be, doubtless a case can be made out for one or other of these implausible solutions.[1]

---

1 There are even less plausible solutions than these. According to some generative

What the example suffices to show is that there is literally no idiosyncrasy of spelling (English or other) that could *not* be accommodated somehow or other in this way; i.e. by construing a sequence of letters as the orthographic sign of a sound already identified as its partner in the spoken form. This is what happens when the assumption that letters *must* represent sounds is carried to its logical conclusion. Writing is not allowed to have 'idle' letters. (That would offend against the Puritan work ethic, scientific comprehensiveness, or some other cultural shibboleth.)

Since the cenemic theorist will admit as counterevidence only letters that have no identifiable partner in the spoken form, and since, as the above example illustrates, it is always possible in alphabetic scripts to find such partners, the cenemic theory of alphabetic scripts is actually vacuous.

That might be counted a pity but harmless, were it not that what is thereby obscured, unfortunately, is the semiological structure of writing systems that are notationally based. As already noted, it would be absurd to explain the survival of 'archaic' spellings by supposing that writers prefer to represent medieval pronunciation rather than their own. It is only slightly less absurd to suppose that what saves these orthographic 'archaisms' from extinction is their phonetic justification in terms of pointless 'digraphs' like *gh* as a variant of *f*.

The fact is that notationally based writing is a flexible and resilient tool because it allows for a variety of structural patterns that can be exploited in different ways. In order to give this fact its theoretical due, it is important to distinguish between the notational identity of a character and its functions as a unit in the script. It is precisely because, in written English, alphabetic letters are units of a notation and not simply phonetic symbols that they have the capacity to fulfil a variety of functions.

One of these functions is indeed related to the pronunciation of words in the spoken language: the *a* of *bat* signals to a reader acquainted with certain English orthoepic practices that this word is pronounced differently from *bit, bet, but*, etc. (although it does not indicate exactly what the difference is – which is one reason why such a spelling can, up to a point, 'survive' regardless of phonetic change and dialectal variation in the spoken language).

On the other hand, letters are also available for a quite different

phonologists, *gh* in words like *right, night*, etc. represents a 'silent' velar fricative |x|, orthographically recognized although never actually pronounced, which really exists somewhere 'in the language' and presumably also in the unobservable cognitive processes of the speaker (N. Chomsky and M. Halle, *The Sound Pattern of English* (New York: Harper & Row, 1968)). It is revealing that the 'discovery' of this ghost sound in English should have been hailed as a triumph of phonological analysis rather than condemned as a ludicrous artifact of formalization. If these phonologists are to be believed, presumably we shall not know that the 'deep' phonology of the word *night* has really changed in English until all writers spell it *nite*. Thus the vagaries of orthography, thanks to the 'insights' of twentieth-century theorists, acquire a status the inventors of the alphabet never dreamed of.

semiological function; namely, word identification. Configurations of letters may form patterns which are related to pronunciation only indirectly, as in *eight*. Sometimes these configurations are a reliable guide at least to rhyme (*eight* : *freight*), but not always (*rough* : *cough*). They do nevertheless tend to establish consistent patterns at the syllabic level over the vocabulary as a whole.

Saussure came close to recognizing these multiple possibilities of structuring (as his extensive but unpublished work on anagrams amply demonstrates). What prevented him from according these possibilities any theoretical recognition in linguistics was his conviction that alphabetic writing existed merely in order to identify minimal segments in the *signifiant*. Thus he could cite French *oiseau* as an example of a spelling in which 'not one of the sounds of the spoken word (*wazo*) is represented by its appropriate sign'.[2] But this already presupposes that the word 'ought' to be written *wazo*.

Semiologically, this latter assumption has no justification; but, worse still, it obscures the fact that *oiseau* conforms perfectly to certain syllabic patterns in French orthography: for example, (i) *oiseau, oisif, oiseux, Oise, toise, ardoise*, etc.; (ii) *oiseau, beau, eau, peau, sceau*, etc. The irony is that if Saussure had seen this he could have cited it to show that a *signifiant* can be written in either of two ways in French: phonemically or syllabically. But that, in effect, would have required conceding that the alphabet has a different semiological status from that which Saussure had assigned to it; in other words, conceding that it is a notation, not a set of independent phonetic symbols.

In terms of integrational analysis, however, this is only one aspect of the semiological structure of the spelling *oiseau*; i.e. that which corresponds to integrating the activities of scanning a text and reading it aloud. It is irrelevant to a reader who has no interest in the pronunciation, but merely wishes to comprehend what is written down. Again, oddly enough, Saussure missed a point which, as a structuralist, he might have been expected not merely to see but to make a great deal of. For on the semantic level *oiseau* fits into at least two lexical paradigms or (in Saussure's terminology) 'associative series': (iii) *oiseau, oiselle, oisellerie, oisillon, oiselet, oiseleur, oiselier*; (iv) *oiseau, corbeau, moineau, bécasseau, étourneau, vanneau*. And in the latter case *oiseau* stands as the semantically superordinate term to all the others.

These graphic patterns exist in the written language, *irrespective of how the words are pronounced*. They are not directly derived from the notational structure itself (i.e. in the way that the place of *33* in the series *3, 33, 333,* . . . is), but nevertheless they depend on the fact that the alphabetic letters are notational and are thus free to function semiologically in more than one way.

This freedom is perhaps most obviously exploited in Western writing by

2   F. de Saussure, *Cours de linguistique générale*, 2nd edn (Paris: Payot, 1922), p. 52.

devices such as anagrams, acrostics and eye-rhymes, usually frowned upon as too trivial for use by serious writers. But this marginalization tells us more about the concept of 'literature' in Western culture than it does about the structure of its writing systems. Anyone who wishes to examine the latter would do better to look at modern advertising material than scrutinize the published works of canonized poets or novelists.

There are, however, writing systems which make a more systematic use of their notational possibilities. Classical Tibetan, as noted earlier (Ch. 9), organizes its written text in a way which is simultaneously 'alphabetic' and 'syllabic' (in Saussurean terms). That is to say, the way the Tibetan graphic unit is arranged is not a direct reflection of the sequence of sounds within the syllable; yet the latter can be derived from the former. Integrationally, this distinction corresponds to two possible processing strategies for the reader. It is possible to read aloud correctly merely by recognizing the global configuration of the graphic syllable. But this strategy will break down if an unfamiliar syllable is encountered. At that point it becomes necessary to understand the internal structure of the configuration in order to arrive at its pronunciation.

Something similar applies in European written languages. (Saussure acknowledged this in his lectures,[3] but his remarks on the subject did not survive into the published text of the *Cours de linguistique générale*.) The difference is that European readers have to guess the pronunciation of unfamiliar words on the basis of analogy, because there is no rigid system of the Tibetan type to guide them. (Hence mistakes like pronouncing *misled* as if it were the past participle of a verb *to mizzle*, and *awry* as if it rhymed with *glory*.) Again, what Saussure did not recognize – or was unwilling to admit – are the theoretical implications of such mistakes and of the dual reading strategy in general. The most important of these implications is that there must be more than one semiological structuring operative in the text; i.e. more than one way in which the reader can derive a written sign from the written form.

---

3   E. Komatsu and R. Harris (eds), *F. de Saussure, Troisième cours de linguistique générale (1910–1911)* (Oxford: Pergamon, 1993), p. 64.

Part IV

Topics in the theory of written communication

Chapter 17

The writing surface

The difference between an integrational and a structuralist semiology of writing is nowhere more evident than in the analysis of how combinations of written signs may be articulated to form a written message.

A structuralist approach takes as its point of departure some given combination of forms: it starts from a decontextualized abstraction already waiting, as it were, to be written down. An integrational approach, on the contrary, starts with the blank surface, considered as the essential point of contact between writer and reader. Whatever integration there may be between the activities of these two needs the surface as the locus for that integration.

It follows that the semiological surface is not necessarily a surface in the physical sense, although in many cases it is that as well. (But it may be simply an area in which forms are assembled for processing by the reader.)

*   *   *

From an integrational point of view, the surface is not semiologically inert or valueless. It makes its contribution to the significance of what is written, and it may do this in various ways. For instance, it may – or may not – be prepared in advance with a view to receiving a written message. If prepared, it may also be prepared in such a way as to indicate a certain order of processing (recto and verso of a document, for example).[1] Thus the preparation of the surface counts as one of the integrated activities linking writer to reader, even though the individual who prepares the surface may not be the same person as the individual who eventually inscribes a text upon it.

Furthermore, the semiological relationship of surface to text may be very

---

1   In cuneiform writing, the tablet is usually prepared so that the front is flat and the back convex. This is an integrational feature related simultaneously to the activities of scribe and reader. The flat side was inscribed first, and the tablet could then be turned over to inscribe the other side without pressure distorting the marks on the front. By the same feature, the reader can immediately tell which is the recto and which is the verso. See C.B.F. Walker, *Cuneiform* (London: British Museum, 1987), p. 22.

different in different cases. At least three possibilities need to be distinguished.

1 The text determines the selection of the surface (because it would not make sense – or would make different sense – on any other surface). The activist who wishes to daub a slogan of protest on the residence of a particular politician must make sure he or she gets the address right.
2 The text presupposes certain physical properties of the surface (because a surface with different physical properties would vitiate the message inscribed on it). Tape measures are not made of elastic, and foot rulers require a surface having at least one dimension of 12 inches.
3 The text functions as a comment on the surface it occupies. Perhaps the most remarkable example of this in the history of writing is provided by the Chinese oracle bones of the Shang dynasty, where the surface itself constitutes a pyromantic 'text', which the writing serves to explain. [2]

* * *

The selection of a suitable surface is subject to biomechanical constraints. For instance, it must be a surface that allows the production of written forms with the writing implements or writing processes available; it must be a surface visible or otherwise accessible, at the appropriate time, to the reader or readers, etc. These and similar considerations impose a preliminary set of circumstantial restrictions.

The selection of a surface is also subject to various macrosocial constraints. In most literate societies, messages cannot be written just anywhere. In the public domain, there is usually quite a strict set of correlations between the right to use certain available surfaces and the organization of social power.[3] Graffiti on walls do not have the same status as carved texts on monuments. *Where* a text appears may affect the question of its validity or authority, particularly when different versions of a text are preserved in different places. The selection of particular materials for the preparation of a writing surface may have other macrosocial implications, depending on the rarity, quality, costliness, etc. of the materials in question.

Subject always to these biomechanical and macrosocial considerations, the primary semiological function of the writing surface *vis-à-vis* the written message is to provide a basis for the organization of graphic space.

In this respect, the surface plays a role analogous to that of other physical structures which serve to articulate variable combinations of signs; for example, the frame and wires of an abacus which hold in place the individual beads whose positions relative to one another signify the total accumulated. Without the frame and wires, the beads would have no

2   D.N. Keightley, *Sources of Shang History: The Oracle-Bone Inscriptions of Bronze Age China* (Berkeley: University of California Press, 1978).
3   M. Corbier, 'L'écriture dans l'espace publique romain', *L'Urbs. Espace urbain et histoire* (Rome: Ecole française de Rome, 1987), pp. 27–60.

positions to take up. Similarly, without the writing surface the written characters would have no graphic space to occupy.

The neglect of a syntagmatics of writing in both traditional and modern linguistics is due mainly to the assumption that the way written signs are combined on a surface is simply a direct copy in visual terms of the way oral signs are combined in speech. Consequently, a separate syntagmatics for the written sign would be otiose: the 'grammar' of a sentence such as *Brutus killed Caesar* is deemed to remain the same, regardless of whether the sentence is spoken or written. So whatever emerges as an account of the syntagmatics of the spoken sentence will also do duty, on this view, for its written counterpart.

Some theorists even insist on this equivalence to the extent of using the term *linear* to describe both the temporal organization of sound sequences in speech and the relationship of graphic signs to one another on a surface. Nothing could be more misguided: it is an open invitation to confusion. Linearity is thus conflated with alignment (see Ch. 18). Such a conflation amounts to ignoring the semiological function of the surface altogether.

From an integrational point of view, there can be no question of any simple 'transposition' of the properties of auditory signs into a visual mode. The biomechanical factors involved in the two forms of communication are totally different. Hearing is not seeing. Quite simply, there is no auditory equivalent of a surface.

Except in one type of case (to be dealt with immediately below), speech communication does not result in the physical marking of durable objects. This difference *eo ipso* drives a semiological wedge between speech and writing. That wedge is the surface.

The exception referred to above is provided by the modern technologies of sound recording. Here we find indeed an interesting analogy, as Oxford's first professor of anthropology noted in 1881, when he observed that the primitive conception of the written document as a 'talking chip' reminds one of

> the modern invention of the phonograph, where the actual sound spoken into the vibrating diaphragm marks indentations in the travelling strip of tinfoil, by which the diaphragm can be afterwards caused to repeat the vibrations and re-utter the sound. When one listens to the tones coming forth from the strip of foil, the South Sea Islander's fancy of the talking chip seems hardly unreasonable.[4]

Tylor made this comment only four years after Edison perfected his system of sound recording. The comparison raises a legitimate question: is the gramophone record writing? To dismiss the matter on the ground that current usage does not sanction including gramophone records in the class

---

4 E.B. Tylor, *Anthropology* (London: Macmillan, 1881), Ch. VII, p. 181.

of objects designated by the term *written texts* is not a semiological answer. On the contrary, it is a refusal to give one.

Neither Saussure nor Peirce confronts the question directly. But it could be argued that if we are to construe writing as a 'silent' but durable representation of speech, then the physical 'indentations' of the wax disc or metal strip constitute a form of writing *par excellence*, and even in Peircian terms an iconic sign.

The integrationist answer to the question is clear: such indentations would indeed be writing if only the human eye or some other organ were biomechanically capable of reading them. But if that were actually the case, then our whole concept of the relationship between forms of communication would be different. That is to say, if we could inspect a gramophone record and read the configurations of the wax surface just as we read the marks on this page, then there would be a good semiological argument for saying that Thomas Edison invented a new form of writing.

As it is, however, the surface of the record or the metal strip is not a writing surface, even though its semiological function is in some respects comparable to that of the page or the wax tablet.

*   *   *

That the persistent use of a certain type of writing surface may have long-term consequences for the development of written forms in a given writing system is widely acknowledged. It is in part what underlies Gelb's general distinction between 'cursive' and 'monumental' writing. Cursive writing is defined as 'a quick and superficial form of writing used for daily practical purposes' as opposed to 'a careful form of writing normally found on monuments and used for official display purposes'.[5] By 'superficial' here, Gelb presumably means that cursive writing lacks the three-dimensional characteristics associated with carving in stone and other materials, although it is worth pointing out that at least in Sumer, where the predominant material was clay, writing was from the earliest times three-dimensional. The best-known case of successively derived cursive forms of writing is that of Egypt, where hieroglyphic writing remained the primary monumental form for more than 3,000 years, but was simplified to give hieratic for use in business and administrative documents, which in turn was later simplified to give demotic. Even here, however, the distinction is not absolute. Hieratic occasionally appears on monuments, while demotic is one of the three scripts found on the Rosetta stone.

A different example of the influence of the writing surface on the written forms is provided by the runic alphabet, where the noticeable absence of curved strokes and horizontal strokes is attributed to the fact that the script

---

5 I.J. Gelb, *A Study of Writing* (Chicago: University of Chicago Press, 1952; rev. edn 1963), pp. 249, 250.

was designed for incision in wood. Vertical strokes were cut at right angles to the grain and slanting strokes across it.[6]

It has been argued that in Europe, until at least the end of the thirteenth century, 'the writing habits ingrained in youth by learning to write on a wax tablet were maintained and reinforced by the continued use through maturity of the wax tablet as the primary drafting medium'.[7]

The rounded shape of characters in Oriya script is attributed to the fact that writing on talipot palm leaves with an iron stylus forced scribes to abandon the horizontal *matra* of Devanagari, because it was difficult to cut straight lines in the direction of the fibre without splitting the leaf.[8]

In all these cases biomechanical factors are clearly involved, facilitating certain developments and inhibiting others. The systematic study of such matters belongs under a *theory of writing techniques* (see Ch. 3).

Another phenomenon of which the history of writing provides countless examples concerns the selection of a particularly difficult surface for the inscription of a text. Usually the biomechanical challenge most favoured by calligraphers is that of miniaturization. Among many astonishing feats, one which perhaps stands out is the inscription of the whole of the Koran on the shell of a single hen's egg.[9]

*   *   *

Turning back now to the comparison between speech and writing, let us see why the syntagmatics of the two are irreducibly different.

Consider the following graphic possibilities:

(i)

      BRUTUS

       KILLED

        CAESAR

(ii)

```
B
R   K
U   I   C
T   L   A
U   L   E
S   E   S
    D   A
    R
```

(iii)

       CAESAR

      KILLED

     BRUTUS

---

6 R.I. Page, *Runes* (London: British Museum, 1987), p. 8.

7 R.H. Rouse and M.A. Rouse, 'Wax tablets', *Language & Communication*, 9, 2/3 (1989), p. 184.

8 D. Diringer, *The Alphabet*, 2nd edn (London: Hutchinson, 1949), pp. 365–6.

9 Y.H. Safadi, *Islamic Calligraphy* (London: Thames & Hudson, 1978), p. 30.

Items (i) and (ii) are at first sight unproblematic if we allow for equivalences between horizontal and vertical alignment. But (iii) presents an ambiguity. We no longer know whether to read from top to bottom or left to right. Worse still, neither reading takes obvious precedence over the other: the organization of graphic space keeps both possibilities in play.

The point here is not how we decide – if we do – whether one reading of (iii) is to be preferred to the other. What is more important is to realize that this is a graphic ambiguity that has no counterpart in the structure of speech. And the reason for this is that writing involves the display of graphic forms on a surface.

Alert readers may suspect that a visual trick is being played on them here. The presentation of (iii) as a conundrum involves juggling with the usual Western expectations about the graphic organization of alphabetic writing. But those readers whose perspicuity matches their alertness will also see that subverting their alphabetic expectations is simply a way of drawing attention to the fact that surfaces make available graphic configurations which are biomechanically impossible in the spoken mode.

This fact becomes of special interest to the semiologist when it is exploited to produce signs which are unique to writing. The case of pattern poetry has already been mentioned (Ch. 8). Scholars who have studied this genre distinguish, rightly, between cases in which the arrangement of text on a surface is merely subject to visually decorative shaping and those in which, as Ernst puts it, the result is 'a graphic figure which in relation to the verbal utterance has both a mimetic and symbolic function'.[10] Semiologically, the two are quite different. The former is simply a contingent use of written forms to create a non-verbal graphic image: it is a kind of scriptorial collage. The latter is a case of semiological syncretism, in which the choices involved in the selection of written forms and visual image are interdependent, and their interdependence contributes to what the resultant whole signifies.

Even more interesting to the semiologist is the phenomenon of interdependent syntagmatics. This involves the use of a surface to construct textual arrangements which feature characters having a dual syntagmatic

Figure 17.1 Alphabetic polyglyph.

10   Ulrich Ernst, 'The figured poem: towards a definition of genre', *Visible Language*, xx, 1 (1986), p. 9.

role within the text itself. To read such a text, the reader has to reckon not only with the possibility of signs functioning simultaneously as emblems and tokens, but additionally as playing both roles in syntagmatically different scannings. Such signs may be termed *polyglyphs*.

The use of polyglyphs is widely exploited in modern advertising (Fig. 17.1), but it has a long ancestry in the history of writing.

Use of the polyglyph makes it possible to articulate two messages by means of a single string of characters. A simple example is the car plate

LoUiSiAna

but the device has also been employed more extensively in literary compositions.

Recognition of the polyglyph as a special written sign is widely attested in different cultures by the development of poetic forms and games of various kinds based specifically upon it. The systematic use of polyglyphs is often associated with magical, hermetic or religious values, as in the case of the famous Sator word square.[11]

```
R  O  T  A  S
O  P  E  R  A
T  E  N  E  T
A  R  E  P  O
S  A  T  O  R
```

Polyglyphs are not associated only with alphabetic writing. In China we find the circular poem (Fig. 17.2).

Figure 17.2 Chinese polyglyphic writing.

11 See Heinz Hofman's article 'Sator-quadrat' in Pauly/Wissowa, *Realencyclopädie* (Munich: Druckenmüller, 1978) suppl. vol. 15, pp. 478–565.

Herbert Franke analyses this particular example as a composition utilizing only sixteen characters, nevertheless yielding a poem of twenty-eight
words with four lines of seven words each. The syntagmatics is based on
repeating for each line the last three words of the preceding line. The last
words of the first, second and fourth lines rhyme, as do the first words of
the fourth, third and fifth lines. The poem is also a palindrome.[12]

In all these cases the polyglyph is made possible by exploiting the
semiological possibilities of the surface. One counterpart of this in drawing,
which likewise deploys marks on a surface, is the utilization by the artist of a
single line which functions simultaneously as the boundary of two different
figures. This gives rise to the visual phenomenon Rudolph Arnheim calls
'contour rivalry'.[13] Systematically exploited, it produces 'illusions' such as
the Necker cube (Fig. 17.3).

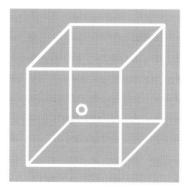

Figure 17.3 Necker cube.

The point to be noted here is that, as in the written examples discussed
above, these are essentially surface-dependent phenomena. When the
Necker cube is constructed as a three-dimensional model, the 'illusion'
vanishes. Similarly, when the Sator word square is read aloud, its graphic
'magic' disappears.

---

12   Herbert Franke, 'Chinese patterned texts', *Visible Language* XX, 1 (1986), pp. 96–108.
13   Rudolph Arnheim, *Art and Visual Perception*, new edn (Berkeley: University of California
Press, 1974), pp. 223ff.

Chapter 18

Graphic space

Every written text needs a graphic space in which to be situated for purposes of reading. This space may or may not be shared with other signs which are not forms of writing.

The determination of graphic space in which a text is situated yields a division within the text between (i) external and (ii) internal syntagmatics.

External syntagmatics covers the various relationships which may obtain between the written forms and items or events to which they are significantly connected in the space outside (i.e. that space within which the 'graphic space' itself is situated). A simple example is the finger-post road sign which displays a place name on a rectangular arm pointing one way. From this, the reader understands that the place identified by the written form is located in a certain direction. If the orientation of the road sign were altered (e.g. by rotating the vertical support through 180 degrees), the message would be different, even though the written form and its position in the graphic space provided by the surface of the road sign were not altered in any particular. (The reader would, as a result of the rotation, understand that the place in question was situated in the opposite direction.)

Internal syntagmatics relates to the disposition of written forms relative to one another and to other forms within the same graphic space. Thus the arrangement of lines of writing on a page such as this pertains to the internal syntagmatics of the text. Within the same graphic space, written forms may be related significantly to diagrams, drawings, illustrations, etc. In Plate 14, the relation between picture and caption belongs to the internal syntagmatics of the graphic space.

In more complex cases, the arrangement of two or more graphic spaces relative to one another may have a signification which relates to the external syntagmatics of their juxtaposition. Thus a right–left reversal of the two names in Plate 15 would indicate a corresponding difference in the spatial relationship between Exeter Road and High Street.

The question of the *direction* of writing in a text (Ch. 19) is a question of internal syntagmatics. Direction is not to be confused with *alignment.* The sequence of characters

$$K J I F P P J T$$

may be read in either of two directions (left-to-right or right-to-left), but in either case their alignment remains the same. A different alignment of the same set of characters would be

K
J
I
F
P
P
J
T

Both alignment and direction have implications for the processing of a written text.

Alignment is commonly used to pair off corresponding sets of written forms within the graphic space, as in

1 @ 5.95	5.95
Subtotal	5.95
Discountable	5.95
10%	0.59
Subtotal	5.36

This simple formula for the utilization of graphic space is ubiquitous in lists of all kinds.[1] Alignment is used in more sophisticated ways in tabular writing (Ch. 20). It can also be used to articulate the external syntagmatics of a text. For example, on a seating plan for a formal dinner, the alignment of names will usually indicate which guests are seated opposite one other. In a case like

12 D. AISLE
E. CENTER
F. WINDOW

where the notice is positioned directly above the relevant row of seats in the aircraft, we see a systematic use of multiple alignment involving both internal and external syntagmatics.

Internal and external syntagmatics may also combine to confer significa-tion on a certain graphic arrangement within the graphic space. For example, the fact that on a signpost place names are listed in a certain order may indicate their *relative* distance from the signpost itself, even though no specific distances are mentioned.

1 On lists as a form of writing, the *locus classicus* is now the chapter 'What's in a list?', in Jack Goody, *The Domestication of the Savage Mind* (Cambridge: Cambridge University Press, 1977).

Given the surface as a basis for articulating graphic space, it is clear that writing may exploit the semiological possibilities in a variety of ways.

The surface may be used to provide either a two-dimensional or a three-dimensional graphic space. Many historians of writing appear to make the tacit assumption that written forms are two-dimensional configurations, i.e. the presence of an additional layer of paint, ink or pigment, or the occurrence of indentation, are ignored. But in various types of context these features may be semiologically relevant.

In the case of braille, the three-dimensional organization of graphic space is biomechanically indispensable. In many forms of monumental writing it is used as a stylistic feature. In deliberate forms of palimpsest, it is utilized to indicate that an earlier message has been superseded by a later one (Plate 3). In early Sumerian, it may even be used to make a distinction between two written characters: the numeral for 'sixty' being made by pressing the round end of the stylus vertically into the wet clay, while the numeral for 'one' is made by varying the angle of impression.[2] (The result in the latter case is an indented 'half-moon' shape, usually transcribed by Western scholars as a semi-circle.) In Chinese writing, the order of strokes demanded in correct calligraphy is, in part at least, determined by the fact that the result can be seen as a three-dimensional configuration by the trained eye, just as in painting.

As noted earlier (Ch. 13), the basic difference between the way a script is used to record information and the way a chart is used to record information hinges on the utilization of graphic space. The chart relies on having the space divided up in some predetermined way, so that what a graphic form signifies depends wholly or partly on the particular division it occupies within that space. Maps and diagrams drawn to scale are based on this principle. That is what makes it possible, for example, to calculate the distance between two geographical points by measuring the corresponding distance on the map.

Other applications of the chart principle are diagrams showing how the values of a selected variable (e.g. temperature) vary over a period of time (e.g. the month of March, 1994). In such cases the quantitative values of the two variables are usually plotted orthogonally within the graphic space (e.g. temperature vertically and time horizontally).

When we compare this to the way such information might be presented in writing without the use of a chart, the difference in the organization of graphic space is immediately apparent. Instead of a configuration of points related to the two axes, we should find a series of sentences (i.e. arrays of alphabetical or other scriptorial forms) displayed on the page in a pattern which bears no relation at all to the co-variation of the values in question. Nor would the value of any individual scriptorial form depend on its

---

2   C.B.F. Walker, *Cuneiform* (London: British Museum, 1987), p. 20.

occupying one particular position determined by a calibration of horizontal and vertical axes on the page.

Because of this radically different organization of graphic space, the processing required in the case of the chart and the script would be quite different.

Writing typically operates in a way which does *not* depend on establishing a fixed value for any absolute position in graphic space. Instead, what is sought is the establishment of the *relative* position of any scriptorial form to other forms sharing the graphic space in question. This is the basis of the internal syntagmatics of a written text.

The graphic contrasts exploited in order to do this include (i) proximity, (ii) alignment, (iii) size, (iv) inclination or slant, and (v) colour. Absolute position within the graphic space counts only as a means of articulating these. There is also the case of (vi) superposition or enclosure, which might alternatively be treated as a special instance of (i). This is frequently employed by graphic artists in layout design (Plate 16). It is more rarely used as a regular feature of writing systems, but occurs in Mayan glyphs (Fig. 18.1).

Figure 18.1 Enclosure in Maya writing. Four different ways of writing *chum tun.*

From an integrational point of view, syntagmatic analysis of writing involves explicating the role which these contrasts play in the formation, processing and interpretation of a text.

Thus, for example, the organization of the title page in Plate 17 shows a set of blocks of print, each of which is identified by a series of internal analogies. They are arranged from top to bottom of the page as

(i) REDEFINING LINGUISTICS, (ii) Edited by, (iii) *Hayley G. Davis and Talbot J. Taylor,* (iv) the Routledge logo, and (v) London and New York.

They are arranged to form three separate units within the rectangle of the page, identified visually by being surrounded with areas of blank space. Each of the three units deals with a separate item of information concerning the book in question.

Here we see a form of graphic communication in which the function of compartmentalization has been assumed by analogies which have not been announced in advance to the reader. The reader is thus obliged to construct the internal syntagmatics of the text on the basis of whatever visual clues can be gleaned from the forms presented in the graphic space.

The sophistication required to do this is of a very high order, at least in the contemporary world of graphic design. The reader is expected to pay attention to – or at least to recognize – analogies of direction, size, slant, colour and letter shape. In one sense, these are all substitutes for a cruder method in which the compartmentalization of graphic space was achieved simply by drawing lines round groups of forms.

This cruder stage can be seen in the box divisions of Sumerian writing, where the marked lines enclose syntactic units in the text or separate items inventoried (Plate 18[3]).

So in one sense the history of writing is a history of successive attempts to escape from being imprisoned within a graphic box. But however desperate the attempts, the box – visible or invisible – remains.

Chinese children are still taught to write their characters within the borders of an imaginary square box.[4] The 'boxing' of graphic space is found in cultures as widely separated as those of ancient Egypt and the Maya. In the former case, it is common in monumental writing to find that in the arrangement of hieroglyphs the boxing principle actually takes precedence over the glottic order of forms. W.V. Davies notes:

> Hieroglyphs were not written in linear sequence, one after another, like the letters of an alphabetic script, but were grouped into imaginary squares or rectangles so as to ensure the most harmonious arrangement and to minimize the possibility of unsightly gaps. Such requirements affected the relative size and proportions of individual signs and deter-mined whether a word was written in full or in an abbreviated form. It is not uncommon to find hieroglyphs switched in their order for reasons of better spacing. Indeed 'graphic transposition', as it is called, is virtually the rule for some sign combinations, particularly those in which a bird hieroglyph is written next to a small squat sign or a tall thin one. Many such transpositions were initially designed to make the most effective use of space in columnar inscriptions, but became so standard that they were often retained in horizontal texts as well.[5]

What this means, in integrational terms, is that hieroglyphic syntagmatics is by no means a mere copying of the syntagmatics of speech. *The box is (at*

3 British Museum 116730. C.B.F. Walker, *Cuneiform* (London: British Museum, 1987), pp. 53–4.
4 An explanation of the box division is given in J. Long, *The Art of Chinese Calligraphy* (Poole: Blandford, 1987), pp. 114ff.
5 W.V. Davies, *Egyptian Hieroglyphs* (London: British Museum, 1987), p. 13.

least) two-dimensional. A separate activity is integrated here, involving a visual aesthetic and visual processing which have no basis in speech whatsoever.

The 'line' of modern alphabetic writing and the 'column' of Chinese characters are extensions of the box principle, organized so as to make maximum use of the graphic space available.

One of the universal tendencies observable in the development of writing is towards adopting a distinctive organization of graphic space for different types of written document. In a writing culture, knowing the proper way to set out various kinds of document becomes an indispensable part of the professional expertise of the secretary or amanuensis.

From an integrational point of view, it is relevant to note that the internal organization of graphic space adopted often corresponds to different activities to be integrated. Thus

```
        John Smith Esq.
    14 Hurlingham Gardens
        Bristol
        England
```

is typical of the layout commonly found in setting out addresses on envelopes (although details of the practice vary in different countries). The rationale of this spacing corresponds quite distinctly to different activities integrated; that is to say, to different phases in the transmission and delivery of the letter. These activities are in fact carried out by a series of different individuals at different times and places – from the time the letter is posted to the time it reaches the hands of John Smith. Each line of the address is, in effect, meant for a different reader. Thus the envelope provides another example of internal and external syntagmatics combining to shape the written form adopted.

Even when the written forms of a text are glottic forms, the availability of contrasts not available in speech may be exploited to produce a syntagmatics which is quite different from that of the corresponding spoken words. For instance, as in the case of Egyptian hieroglyphs, the order of the written forms may not correspond to the spoken sequence (Plate 4).

The basic difference between writing and drawing (together with painting, etching and related graphic arts) also hinges on the organization of graphic space. No one mistakes even a child's drawing of a cat for a written description of a cat. Why is that?

It is not that the drawing operates in the same way as a chart (i.e. by assigning a predetermined value to any given location in graphic space). Like writing, the drawing of the cat seeks to establish relative rather than absolute positions in space, and hence relative rather than absolute relations between the graphic configurations it deploys. We have to see that *this* line is the cat's tail, and therefore need to see it as related to the shape depicting the cat's body; that *this* line is the cat's ear, and bears a certain relation to the shape depicting the cat's head, etc. This is, indeed, a kind of visual syntagmatics.

How it differs from writing turns on the fact that the visual processing we require to 'see' the drawn figure is biomechanically related to that required to see the cat itself; but is quite different from that required to read any description of the animal.

An indirect confirmation of the above analyses is provided by the observation that when writing is consciously pushed in the direction of drawing, what we find is a deliberate interference with the analogies that normally sustain the organization of a written text: those based on contrasts of proximity, alignment, size, inclination and colour. All of these are systematically subverted in the example of Dadaist 'anti-writing' presented in Plate 7.

Chapter 19

Direction

The concept of direction ('left-to-right', 'top-to-bottom', etc.) is a great source of confusion in discussions of writing. Are we talking about the reader, or the writer, or the orientation of the writing surface? An integrational approach can not only remove this confusion but show what semiological role directionality plays in the constitution of written texts.

Children brought up in the European educational tradition are often dimly aware that in certain other cultures people write 'back to front' or 'the wrong way round'. These notions are not unrelated to the fact that in their own writing they have been corrected when they confuse *b* with *d*, *p* with *q*, etc. In other words, they have been brought up to believe that, in both writing and reading, there is only one right place to start on the page and one correct order of proceeding from there on, and that this determines the proper configuration of the individual characters of the writing system they are being taught.

As a result, they are often surprised and puzzled when it is pointed out to them that it is perfectly possible – although not 'easy' (i.e. biomechanically very different) – to learn to read a page up-side down or to write a sentence starting at the right and finishing at the left.

Puerile perplexities of this order nevertheless point to a genuine semiological complexity in the graphic organization of the written sign (which, again, has no counterpart in corresponding speech forms[1]). This complexity arises from the fact that the graphic space has more than one dimension and thus permits a variety of possible forming and processing procedures. The issue has been further confused by those linguists who insist that, appearances notwithstanding, all glottic writing is 'linear', just like speech. [2]

Although there are many different writing systems in many different

---

1 Anyone who has experimented with a tape recorder or a sound spectrograph will rapidly become convinced that 'talking backwards' is a biomechanical impossibility, at least for the ordinary mortal. (There is an additional logical puzzle as to what 'talking backwards' would actually consist in; but this cannot be pursued here.)

2 E.g. F. de Saussure: see *Cours de linguistique générale*, 2nd edn (Paris: Payot, 1922), p. 103.

countries, writing has its own geometry. It has nothing to do with what language is being written. It is based on a simple fact: namely, that writing starts with a graphic space. In that space written forms have to be arranged in such a way that they can be read.

Any two-dimensional blank space can be considered as comprising an imaginary grid of squares waiting to be 'filled in'. Each square, let us suppose, is just large enough to accommodate a single character. Now the problem of direction is not that of determining the order in which the squares are actually filled in by the writer, nor that of determining the order in which they are actually picked out by the eye of the reader. *Direction* is a semiological concept, not a biomechanical concept, and as such pertains to the structure of the message. It makes no difference whether the individual writer sets down the forms in this sequence or that (any more than it matters whether an artist begins by painting the grapes or the apple or the oysters in his still life). What matters, as in the case of the still life, is that the forms shall be finally arranged in such a way as to articulate the desired composition.

Nevertheless, as soon becomes apparent in any analysis of the organization of graphic space, any solution to the semiological problem of direction will have biomechanical implications. When one considers the features of directionality found in traditional writing systems it is difficult to resist the conclusion that biomechanical factors have played an important role.

For simplicity of exposition, it will be convenient to imagine a hypothetical writer whose invariable practice it is to set down the forms in an order which corresponds to the internal syntagmatics of his text. Such a writer has available, in principle, a very large number of choices. In order to fill the graphic space, he must make a start *somewhere*. Where he starts will limit the options available for carrying on. Assuming a two-dimensional spatial grid, the maximum number of options will be available if the start is made somewhere in the middle of the space, i.e. if he writes the first character in one of the central squares of the grid.

Proceeding from there, a natural principle to adopt would be to place the second sign immediately adjacent to the first. (If no order as such is semiologically relevant – that is, if the text has no internal syntagmatics – then it does not matter where the second sign stands in relation to the first, unless this is determined by *external* syntagmatics. Otherwise, the signs may be arranged anywhere in the space, and direction does not enter into the semiological organization of the text.)

It is precisely at this point – in considering where the second form shall stand in relation to the first – that the question of direction first arises. Except in cryptography (and the exception is revealing), the principle of immediate proximity is universally employed in glottic writing. But it poses an obvious problem: i.e. how to determine in which of the available proximate squares to place the 'next' character.

Furthermore, since the same problem will recur for the third character, and again for the fourth, and so on *ad infinitum*, there is an obvious (biomechanical) advantage, both for the writer and for the reader, in adopting a solution which, so far as possible, minimizes the difficulty of identifying which the 'next' square is.

In other words, the optimum principle will be one which eliminates as many as possible of the many alternatives and ambiguities which would otherwise arise in plotting a consecutive path through the two-dimensional grid.

The question of where the path starts now becomes of crucial importance. For no glottic writing system has so far been devised which would allow us to proceed, as the fancy takes us, in either direction along it. (This, it should be noted, is not – or not ultimately – a biomechanical but a semiological restriction. One might perhaps be able to train oneself to read English from right to left – the enterprise would be difficult and quite pointless, but not, one suspects, impossible. But even if successful, this feat of processing would then require the reader to 'reverse' the information acquired in order to make sense of it. In other words, it is not so much that one could not scan the sentence *Brutus killed Caesar* backwards, as that, having done so, it would then be necessary to convert *Caesar killed Brutus* back into *Brutus killed Caesar*. Or else learn to do the subject–object transpositions *en route*. The perversity involved is analogous to training oneself to be able to recognize photographs of people from the negative image, in preference to studying the positive print.)

Reverting now to the question of where the path starts, one of the interesting things revealed by the history of writing is that, as far as we know, no traditional system of glottic writing was ever developed on the basis of putting Sign No. 1 in the middle of the graphic space. Why not?

At least three reasons may be suggested. First, when a grid of any size is filled in, an initial central square becomes more difficult to pick out than one located in any of the four corners. (A spiral configuration obviates this difficulty, but has its own problems: see below.) Second, for any initial square situated in the interior of the grid, there will be eight rival candidates for the position of 'next' square according to the principle of immediate proximity, five candidates if the initial square is somewhere along one edge, but only three if the initial square is situated in a corner. Third, if a start is made in the middle, the path will at some point have to loop back on itself, unless areas of the available graphic space are to be wasted (i.e. left blank).

Although it is perfectly possible to utilize the graphic space fully by opting for a spiral path (beginning in the centre and working out, or else beginning at the periphery and working in) this solution will require the reader to be continually shifting the orientation of the surface, or else require the ability to recognize the characters 'any way up', or else demand a constant adjustment in the scanning track which the eye follows. (If glottic writing were really 'linear', as some theorists maintain, the spiral would be the principle of textual organization *par excellence*.)

The directionality followed by most traditional writing systems is based on alignment (i.e. the adoption of the 'straight line' – shortest distance between two points – as a basis for the path through the grid). This has the additional advantage of allowing the path to start in a corner. But it still leaves various geometrical possibilities open. Any one of four corners may be chosen as the starting point, and the 'straight lines' may run vertically, horizontally or diagonally.

No known writing system chooses the diagonal option, and this is doubtless related to the problem of filling the graphic space. (If the first line of writing follows one of the major diagonals, how does one effect the transition between opposite triangles of the graphic space?)

Eliminating the diagonal option leaves horizontal lines ('rows') and vertical lines ('columns'). Both are sequences of adjacent squares in the two-dimensional grid.

Here we encounter the second 'directional' problem a writing system has to solve. There is the direction which links squares within the row or the column, and there is the direction followed by the rows or columns relative to one another. And these two 'directions' are geometrically independent. That is: it is possible to have rows going from top to bottom or bottom to top, independently of whether the internal path goes from left to right or right to left. And *mutatis mutandis* for columns.

But the geometry is more complicated still, for the combination of these two directions produces a third. This is the direction obtained by drawing a straight line between the initial square on the grid and the final square. In the European tradition, writing starts at the top left and finishes at the bottom right. In the Chinese tradition, writing starts at the top right and finishes at the bottom left.

No major traditional writing system goes from bottom right to top left, or from bottom left to top right. The reason for this is again in all probability biomechanical: any bottom–up system will have the disadvantage of forcing the writer's hand to conceal part of what has been written previously. If ink or some liquid pigment is being used for writing, there is the additional problem of smudging the text.

All 'straight line' systems, however, encounter a directional problem when the writer's first line reaches the edge of the graphic space. Where to go next?

European glottic writing offers a very interesting solution to this problem. What is called a 'line' of text is based on a convention whereby when writing reaches the edge of the graphic space, *instead of continuing the path according to the principle of immediate proximity*, a break is made. A fresh start is made on an adjacent parallel line. This break is not syntagmatically determined. It is purely and simply a question of the organization of graphic space.

('Verse' is distinguished by introducing new lines where they are *not* called for by the distribution of forms in relation to the graphic space available.)

What this does is sacrifice strict continuity, but allow the writer to keep all the characters 'facing the same way'. And this is the third factor involved in directionality. It operates in Chinese writing too, although there the line is a column, not a row.

Curiously, there is no metalinguistic term for this, although it is tempting to call it 'face': i.e. the relationship between horizontal orientation and alignment. In some forms of writing, face depends on the disposition of adjacent non-written signs. On Egyptian monuments, hieroglyphs commonly face the same way as accompanying figures depicted in the same graphic space (Fig. 19.1).

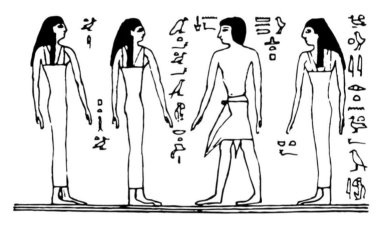

Figure 19.1 Hieroglyphic directionality.

Boustrophedon writing (i.e. alternately from left to right and right to left) may or may not involve a corresponding change of face. In theory, boustrophedon ('as the ox goes') may assume various possible forms: (i) the lines change direction, but nothing else, (ii) both line and face change, (iii) the order of certain groups of characters changes, but there is no change within the group, (iv) the order of groups changes, together with a change of face, etc.

The failure of any form of boustrophedon to survive in a major writing system (despite ample attestation at early stages in the development of scripts in various parts of the world) again points to biomechanical factors which are not as yet clearly understood. That is to say, it seems 'preferable' to have writing going in a uniform direction with no change of face than to have strict continuity but changes of direction when the edges of the graphic space are reached. The question of face, clearly, gives rise to particular problems when a script has different characters which are distinguished mainly by the left–right position of different strokes (as *b* and *d*, *p* and *q*, etc.).

In many parts of the world, we observe an interesting toleration or accommodation between direction and alignment, as if one could be traded off against the other (see Appendix D). Externally, the decision seems to depend on the shape of the graphic space available. The trade-off usually seems to involve swapping left–right rows for top–bottom columns, or vice versa. Whether there is a biomechanical basis for this exchange is as yet unclear.

There is one further directional issue that arises. This concerns the organization of a text spread out over several graphic spaces, as in the composition of the modern book or newspaper. The scroll, the codex, etc. are ways of organizing these relations between graphic spaces, and their adoption in turn requires specific processing activities to be integrated into the reading of a text.

From a Western point of view, Chinese books are printed 'from back to front', as are Arabic newspapers. The rationale turns out to be very simple. If the organization of each page is from top right-hand corner to bottom left, then arranging the pages in the Chinese way makes sense. That is to say, ordering the pages in the Western way would be going against the direction of the lines. It likewise makes sense for Western books to be printed as they are, because that also follows the direction of the lines. So, in spite of appearances, Oriental and Occidental books in fact follow the same integrational principles at all levels.

Chapter 20

Non-glottic writing: mathematics

In traditional accounts of writing, little attention is paid to mathematics and music because the forms of writing established in those fields are regarded as secondary derivatives from glottic writing. This treatment shows a lamentable disregard of semiological criteria and a no less lamentable confusion of the history of writing with the history of languages.

For an integrationist, mathematical and musical texts, as well as choreographic texts, employ quite distinctive types of writing, being based on the integration of entirely different activities and requiring typically different processing procedures.

In the case of mathematics, the salient feature is not that mathematical texts deal mainly with quantifiable information, but rather that their scriptorial structure is designed with a view to integrating various kinds of calculation – a factor usually quite irrelevant to the reading of non-mathematical texts. In order to accommodate this special integrational requirement, mathematics has, over the centuries, developed the syntagmatics of writing in certain quite characteristic ways.

These developments are hardly mentioned in the majority of books on writing. In Gelb's *A Study of Writing*, which claims to be a general survey of the field on a 'comparative–typological' basis, we find that the space devoted to mathematical writing amounts in total to rather less than one page in a book of some 300 pages. This is despite the fact that its author acknowledges mathematics as one of the sciences that could not have evolved to its modern state *without* writing.[1] The reason for this neglect, presumably, is that the form of writing developed by mathematicians falls, as Gelb puts it, 'outside our normal phonetic system of signs'.[2] Leaving aside for the moment the question of whether our 'normal system of signs' actually is phonetic (Ch. 16), the reasoning is puzzling; for one might have thought mathematical writing on that score all the more worthy of attention as

---

1 I.J. Gelb, *A Study of Writing* (Chicago: University of Chicago Press, 1952; rev. edn 1963), pp. 228–9.
2 *Ibid.*, p. 18.

illustrating the way in which writing can become an essential tool in developing new areas of human knowledge that are not phonetically based. Mathematics, seen in this perspective, might arguably be regarded as the field of writing *par excellence.*

Gelb claims that in a typical mathematical formula 'each single sign has or can have an exact correspondence in speech', but the meaning of the formula as a whole is 'conveyed by the sum of the signs in an order and form which do not follow the conventions of normal, phonetic writing'. He apparently fails to see that these abnormal conventions of mathematicians cannot even be understood on the basis of 'normal, phonetic writing' and that mathematical texts, far from being abnormal, constitute a quite separate species of the genus *writing.*

It is in any case misleading to assume that 'an exact correspondence in speech' can be found for each single sign in a mathematical formula. In the first place it is not true, and even if it were true it would be as irrelevant to the written structure of the mathematical formula as the fact that the red and green lights of a traffic signal can be read aloud as 'Stop!' and 'Go!' respectively is to the organization of the traffic-signalling system.

Although we can read out the expression '$\sqrt{2}$' as 'square root of two', this is far from being 'an exact correspondence in speech'. If such a correspondence were available, there would be no need for a combination of four separate spoken words to render a combination of two mathematical signs. Gelb evidently does not distinguish between exact correspondence and rough equivalence.

Similarly, he assimilates the 'principle of positional value' found in mathematical expressions (such as '33', where the two 3s indicate tens and units respectively) to the device sometimes used in Egyptian hieroglyphics whereby the juxtaposition of two signs is used to indicate a missing syllable which has to be inferred from that juxtaposition. (Thus the glyph for 'jar' placed over the glyph for 'water' expresses a syllabic combination that can be read as 'water' + 'under' + 'jar', which sequence in turn corresponds phonetically to the Egyptian word for 'within'.) It hardly needs a mathematician to point out that a visual rebus of this kind has nothing whatsoever to do with the mathematical principle of positional value.

The above observations exhaust Gelb's account of mathematical writing. Given their paucity, it is hardly surprising that Gelb's reader comes away with the impression that mathematicians have made little, if any, contribution to writing, as compared with the Herculean labours of those who devised alphabets and syllabaries.

Quite the contrary impression is given when one reads histories of mathematics. There it becomes apparent that mathematicians were the first thinkers who realized the enormous potential of writing *as writing.* From an integrational perspective, there can be no doubt that this alternative assessment is the right one. For as long as integration with speech remained the predominant concern of writers and the makers of writing systems, it is unlikely that any serious attention would have been paid to the properties of the written sign as such.

Mathematicians were not in this position. They did not have to concern themselves with how their texts would be read aloud. The alphabet itself was a blind alley for mathematics, as it was for music. In Greek and Roman mathematics, alphabetically based numeral systems were a hindrance rather than a help.

Sumerian place notation, the major breakthrough of the ancient world, must have been, as Marvin Powell has pointed out, 'the product of conscious human invention';[3] for there is no way it could have 'evolved' out of the earlier cumbrous system the Sumerians used. One might add that, from a semiological point of view, this invention represents not a development of but a complete break away from any notion that written signs should conform to or mirror the structures of spoken language. To put the point more sharply, place notation *could not have been invented at all* if integration with speech had been the overriding concern of the inventor.

We do not know how the numerical expressions of the new Sumerian place-system notation were read aloud, but it is no more plausible to see the written forms themselves as modelled on expressions already existing in spoken Sumerian than it would be to regard 'one point nought four two' as an expression existing in colloquial English before the introduction of decimal notation by mathematicians. In short, what the historical evidence suggests is that it was the realization that writing does *not* have to be calqued on speech that lay at the heart of this crucial step forward at the end of the third millennium BC.

Exactly the same is true of the next great advance, the invention of a 'zero' symbol, which was devised during the Seleucid period. Here again there is no question of finding a sign for a previously existing spoken form. What was needed was a 'place-holder' to avoid internal ambiguities in the already established place notation, and this was supplied by using a cuneiform character comprising two small wedges placed obliquely.[4] The fact that Seleucid mathematicians did not, as the Arabs later did, extend the use of this place-holder systematically to all positions, but left it out when no confusion was likely, confirms that its invention was initially a solution to a writing problem.[5]

By comparison with the Sumerian, both systems of Greek numerical

---

3   M.A. Powell, Jr, 'The origin of the sexagesimal system: the interaction of language and writing', *Visible Language*, VI, 1, (1972), p. 14.

4   C.B. Boyer, *A History of Mathematics*, 2nd edn (New York: Wiley, 1991), pp. 26–7.

5   In particular, the place-holder was omitted in final position, which seems initially surprising; but this can be seen as corresponding to the modern convention of the 'floating decimal point'. (For discussion, see O. Neugebauer, *The Exact Sciences in Antiquity*, 2nd edn (Providence: Brown University Press, 1957), pp. 20–2.)

Plates

Plate 8 Kinetically integrated signs.

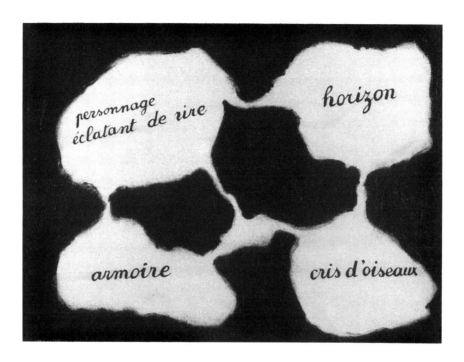

Plate 9 Graphic substitution as a surrealist technique: Magritte's *Le Miroir vivant* (1926).

Plate 10 Scriptorial semantics: Gothic borrowing.

Plate 11 A pseudo-script: mock Oriental.

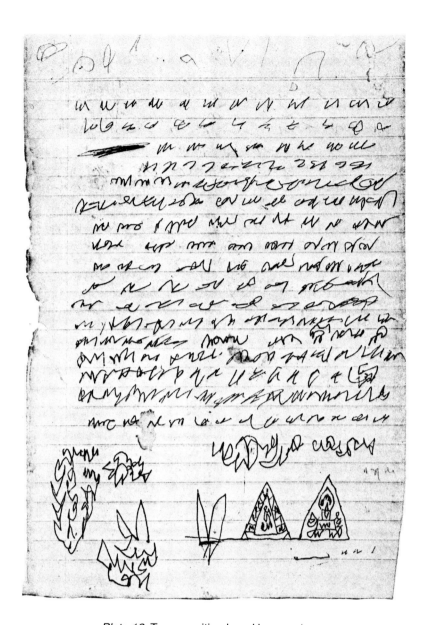

Plate 12 Trance writing by a Hmong *shau*.

Plate 13 Duality of structure: script and notation.

In the art of the 20th century, Boston is best known for figurative and expressionistic painting. The titans of Boston Expressionism during the era of the 1930s through the 1950s were Hyman Bloom, Jack Levine and Karl Zerbe. The German-born Zerbe was a legendary teacher for a generation of artists at the Boston Museum School, such as Henry Schwartz, whose student works from the 1950s and more-recent paintings are the subject of a retrospective exhibition at Gallery Naga through Feb. 26.

For the past two years, Schwartz has been on leave from the Museum School, where he has conveyed the tradition of figurative expressionism to a new generation of artists. The Fuller Museum of Art hosted a major retrospective for the artist several years ago, but this gallery exhibition presents vintage paintings, including a series of student self-portraits that were not

HENRY SCHWARTZ: Room 112, *oil on board, 1982.*

Plate 14 Graphic space: internal syntagmatics.

Plate 15 Graphic space: external syntagmatics.

Plate 16 Enclosure in modern advertising.

REDEFINING LINGUISTICS

Edited by
Hayley G. Davis
and Talbot J. Taylor

London and New York

Plate 17 Internal syntagmatics: analogical differentiation.

Plate 18 Compartmentalization of graphic space: Sumerian tablet.

Plate 19 Alignment variations.

Plate 20 External syntagmatics as a determinant of direction.

notation (the so-called 'Herodianic' and the alphabetic system[6]) were retrograde moves, precisely because they treated written numerical symbols as nothing more than abbreviations for words.[7] Historians of mathematics disagree about which of the two was worse. Cantor thought the Herodianic system better than the alphabetic system that replaced it, and Gow called the alphabetic notation 'a fatal mistake'.[8] Although it had the apparent advantage of economy over the token-iterative Herodianic numerals, its originators seem to have been so obsessed with utilizing all the alphabetic letters available that they failed to see that – to put the point in semiological terms – the structure of the alphabet as an emblematic frame (see Appendix A) actually obscures any arithmetic relations between numbers. Distributing twenty-seven letters over the set of natural numbers from 1 to 999 makes no arithmetic sense at all.

An interesting example of conflict between the structure of the notation and the syntagmatics of the expression system is to be seen in the early hesitation over whether to write the numerals in ascending order (i.e. alphabetical order) or descending order. Thus not only do we find the number '111' written both as PIA and AIP, but even as the muddled compromise PAI.[9]

However, there is one brilliant Greek contribution to mathematics which, although not usually regarded as based on a development in writing, is in fact just that. This is the insight, usually attributed to Pythagoras, which Aristotle describes as 'bringing numbers into the forms of triangle or square'.[10] As Burnet points out, this

> seems to imply the existence at this date, and earlier, of a numerical symbolism quite distinct from the alphabetical notation on the one hand and from the Euclidean representation of numbers by lines on the other. . . . It seems rather that numbers were originally represented by dots arranged in symmetrical and easily recognised patterns, of which the marking of dice or dominoes gives us the best idea.[11]

Such a system would be in origin, clearly, nothing other than a simple set of token-iterative signs for the natural numbers, and the 'dots', as Burnet notes, were doubtless graphic substitutes for pebbles. The genius of Pythagoras – if it was indeed he – lay in developing this simple graphic device into the theory of triangular, square and oblong numbers.

It is of Pythagoras, at any rate, that the anecdote is told concerning the

---

6 T.L. Heath, *A History of Greek Mathematics* (Oxford: Clarendon Press, 1921), pp. 30–7.
7 In fact, the basic Herodianic symbols were just the first letters of the corresponding Greek words for the numbers in question.
8 Heath, *History of Greek Mathematics*, pp. 37–8.
9 *Ibid.*, p. 36.
10 *Metaphysics* N.5, 1092 b 10.
11 J. Burnet, *Early Greek Philosophy* (London: Black, 1948), pp. 100–1.

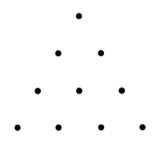

Figure 20.1 Pythagorean *tetraktys*.

student invited to count upwards from 'one'. When he reached 'four', Pythagoras interrupted him and said: 'Do you see? What you take for 4 is 10, a perfect triangle and our oath.'[12] The reference is to the Pythagorean *tetraktys* (Fig. 20.1), which 'represented the number ten as the triangle of four'.[13]

The *tetraktys* is a graphic configuration which takes the Sumerian numeral characters one stage further. The Sumerians had long since hit on the improvement of arranging a token-iterative combination in a pattern that is easily recognizable, instead of a single continuous row[14] (thus showing a high regard for having a reader-friendly set of signs). What the *tetraktys* does is exploit the two-dimensional writing surface for a different purpose, i.e. to arrange the constituent tokens in such a way that the configuration *displays* the relevant numerical relations. Adopting such a graphic device undoubtedly facilitates thinking numerically in a quite different way. Semiologically, what has happened is that a new level of iconicity has been added to the representation of numbers. Whereas a single row of tokens in effect shows the number just as 'one more' or 'one less' than its neighbours in rank order, and reader-friendly configurations of the Sumerian type (Fig. 20.2) show the number as an arbitrary grouping of two or three smaller groups, the Pythagorean symbol reveals at a glance the whole set of properties that characterize – indeed identify – the number.

Patently, it would have been pointless to attempt to bring a Pythagorean type of system into general use for numerical expressions occurring in non-mathematical texts. Nor, probably, would it have served the purposes of everyday accountancy in ancient Greece any better than the alphabetic numerals. Nevertheless, as a development in the history of writing it cannot simply be ignored as if it had never happened.

---

12 Cited in Heath, *History of Greek Mathematics*, p. 77. The text from Lucian is given in I. Thomas, *Greek Mathematical Works*, vol. 1 (Cambridge, Mass.: Harvard University Press; London: Heinemann (Loeb Classical Library), 1939), p. 90. The oath was that of the Pythagorean brotherhood.
13 Burnet, *Early Greek Philosophy*, p. 102.
14 Powell, 'Origin of the sexagesimal system', p. 14.

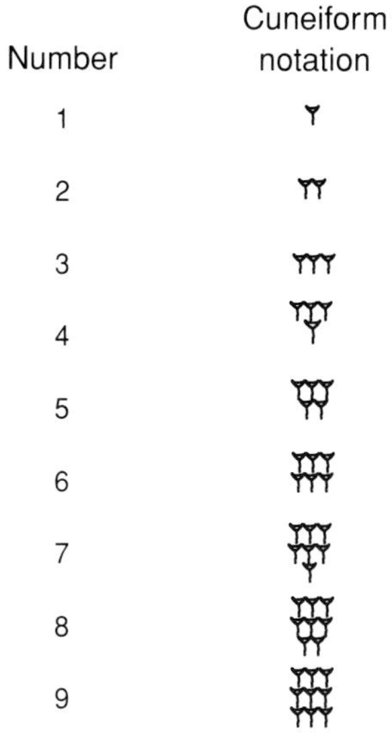

Number	Cuneiform notation
1	Y
2	YY
3	YYY
4	YYY / Y
5	YYY / YY
6	YYY / YYY
7	YYYY / YYY
8	YYYY / YYYY
9	YYYYY / YYYY

Figure 20.2 Cuneiform numerals.

A development of more mundane utility, which was eventually to become part of the mathematical writing system taught to every schoolchild, was likewise based on utilizing the two-dimensional writing surface, but for syntagmatic purposes instead of notation. The modern layout of the simple sum of addition has the (place-notational) Arabic figures arranged in columns:

$$\begin{array}{r} 43 \\ 17 \\ 22 \\ \hline 82 \end{array}$$

Why? Because the activity to be integrated is not simply 'reading' the text but mental calculation based on the rote memorization of 'tables' of equivalences. To facilitate this, the figures are laid out so that the vertical alignment on the page immediately identifies the items to be added in a succession of operations. (It may be noted in passing that the sequence of operations processes the columns from right to left, not from left to right, that is, in the opposite direction to the way the constituent numerals are 'read'.) If the same sum is set out as

$$43 + 17 + 22 = 82$$

there is no comparable visual guide to indicate what has to be added to what. The difference, which seems minimal when there are only two-place figures to be added, is striking when the figures run to six places or more.

Semiologically, the difference between the two scriptorial arrangements is interesting. Setting aside the incorporation of the signs '+' and '=' in the second case, what has happened is that an equivalence has been established between a horizontal alignment and a vertical alignment, maintaining the left-to-right orientation of all figures. Thus, for instance, whereas in the horizontal disposition '3' is identified as meaning 'three ones' by standing to the right of '4' and having no other figure immediately to its right, in the vertical disposition this is reinforced – or doubly marked – by its appearance in the rightmost column.

The point is that this is in fact not an essential feature of the vertical arrangement for purposes of doing the sum. Everything would work out just as well if the units were set out in the left column and the tens in the right. The processing would then go from left to right by columns, instead of from right to left. So in the arrangement as set out above, there is in fact a 'grammatical' rule of agreement which links the semiology of the horizontal arrangement to that of the corresponding vertical arrangement. The integrational advantage of this is obvious. It avoids disturbing the combinatorial composition – that is, the syntagmatics – of the numerals: they do not have to be written 'backwards' in some instances and 'forwards' in others. But this has nothing to do with the principle of place notation as such. Place notation would work equally well if the Arabic numerals were written 'the other way round'.

What this shows is that the integrational 'architecture' of the vertical arrangement is designed to allow for incorporating and facilitating the extra activity of 'adding up', while at the same time preserving the graphic identity of the separate items constituting the addenda.

One might test this by considering what other spatial configurations are possible by using alignment as a semiological device. Obviously, the same result could be obtained by writing out the sum as:

$$4 \ 1 \ 2 : 8$$
$$3 \ 7 \ 2 : 2$$

where one would add the rows from left to right, beginning with the lower (lowest) row and 'carrying over' as usual. The problem with this, clearly enough, is that again it involves varying the 'normal' interpretation of left–right juxtaposition for the Arabic numerals.

It emerges that the classic 'blackboard' arrangement of vertical columns is the only one which preserves intact the visual shape of the Arabic numerals. (There would be nothing to prevent the addition being done from the bottom up, and the total written at the head of the column. What would be odd about *that* is something different altogether; viz. that on a page read from top to bottom the result of the sum would then precede what had to be added – a rather Irish form of arithmetic, to say the least.)

The type of arrangement discussed above is only a special case of a syntagmatics found far more generally in mathematical writing and which may be called *tabular*. The origins of the table can be traced back to Babylonian mathematics. Neugebauer notes that already in the Old Babylonian period we find tables of squares and square roots, cubes and cube roots, sums of squares and cubes needed for the numerical solution of special types of cubic equations, and of exponential functions which were used for the computation of compound interest.[15]

Semiologically, tabular writing must not be confused with the adoption of the chart principle (Ch. 13). In a chart, the whole graphic space is semantically mapped in advance in a uniform way, whereas in tabular writing the meanings depend on syntagmatic relations between co-occurring graphic forms. The difference becomes apparent when we compare (i) a hospital temperature chart, which plots the patient's temperature as a function of time, giving eventually a line traced across a grid to show the ups and downs, with (ii) the table of figures which could display the same information in two parallel columns (but without the iconic visual aid provided by the line on the chart).

The semiological feature of developed tabular writing is the use of graphic space in such a way that *at least two* alignments are simultaneously significant. Thus, in the table of square roots (Fig. 20.3), the significance of each figure in the main body of the text is determined simultaneously by its row and its column.

In lattice multiplication (Fig. 20.4), not only the rows and the columns but also the diagonals are structurally relevant. Furthermore, a single numeral may be written using both horizontal and vertical alignments. (In the example given, the product – 15,504 – obtained by multiplying 456 by 34 is read off the bottom line from left to right followed without a break by the right-hand column from bottom to top.)

The use of tabular writing, in one form or another, is a feature of the indigenous mathematics of such diverse cultures as the Babylonian, the Greek, the Indian, the Egyptian and the Chinese (Fig. 20.5[16]).

Not only is tabular writing a major development of writing *per se*, but its ubiquity suggests, at least to an integrationist, that we are dealing here with a biomechanical universal. In other words, human vision is organized in such a way that a contrast in two-dimensional alignment is selected as the visually effective way to express a semiological pattern in which two separate

15 Neugebauer, *Exact Sciences in Antiquity*, p. 34.
16 This table from the early fourteenth-century *Ssu Yuan Yü Chien* shows what Western mathematicians call the 'Pascal' triangle. It is entitled 'The old method chart of the seven multiplying squares' and tabulates the binomial coefficients up to the eighth power. Boyer, *A History of Mathematics*, p. 208.

x	0	1	2	3	4	5	6	7	8	9
10	1000 3162	1005 3178	1010 3194	1015 3209	1020 3225	1025 3240	1030 3256	1034 3271	1039 3286	1044 3302
11	1049 3317	1054 3332	1058 3347	1063 3362	1068 3376	1072 3391	1077 3406	1082 3421	1086 3435	1091 3450
12	1095 3464	1100 3479	1105 3493	1109 3507	1114 3521	1118 3536	1122 3550	1127 3564	1131 3578	1136 3592
13	1140 3606	1145 3619	1149 3633	1153 3647	1158 3661	1162 3674	1166 3688	1170 3701	1175 3715	1179 3728
14	1183 3742	1187 3755	1192 3768	1196 3782	1200 3795	1204 3808	1208 3821	1212 3834	1217 3847	1221 3860
15	1225 3873	1229 3886	1233 3899	1237 3912	1241 3924	1245 3937	1249 3950	1253 3962	1257 3975	1261 3987
16	1265 4000	1269 4012	1273 4025	1277 4037	1281 4050	1285 4062	1288 4074	1292 4087	1296 4099	1300 4111
17	1304 4123	1308 4135	1311 4147	1315 4159	1319 4171	1323 4183	1327 4195	1330 4207	1334 4219	1338 4231
18	1342 4243	1345 4254	1349 4266	1353 4278	1356 4290	1360 4301	1364 4313	1367 4324	1371 4336	1375 4347
19	1378 4359	1382 4370	1386 4382	1389 4393	1393 4405	1396 4416	1400 4427	1404 4438	1407 4450	1411 4461
20	1414 4472	1418 4483	1421 4494	1425 4506	1428 4517	1432 4528	1435 4539	1439 4550	1442 4561	1446 4572
21	1449 4583	1453 4593	1456 4604	1459 4615	1463 4626	1466 4637	1470 4638	1473 4658	1476 4669	1480 4680
22	1483 4690	1487 4701	1490 4712	1493 4722	1497 4733	1500 4743	1503 4754	1507 4764	1510 4775	1513 4785
23	1517 4796	1520 4806	1523 4817	1526 4827	1530 4837	1533 4848	1536 4858	1539 4868	1543 4879	1546 4889
24	1549 4899	1552 4909	1556 4919	1559 4930	1562 4940	1565 4950	1568 4960	1572 4970	1575 4980	1578 4990
25	1581 5000	1584 5010	1587 5020	1591 5030	1594 5040	1597 5050	1600 5060	1603 5070	1606 5079	1609 5089
26	1612 5099	1616 5109	1619 5119	1622 5128	1625 5138	1628 5148	1631 5158	1634 5167	1637 5177	1640 5187
27	1643 5196	1646 5206	1649 5215	1652 5225	1655 5235	1658 5244	1661 5254	1664 5263	1667 5273	1670 5282
28	1673 5292	1676 5301	1679 5310	1682 5320	1685 5329	1688 5339	1691 5348	1694 5357	1697 5367	1700 5376
29	1703 5385	1706 5394	1709 5404	1712 5413	1715 5422	1718 5431	1720 5441	1723 5450	1726 5459	1729 5468
30	1732 5477	1735 5486	1738 5495	1741 5505	1744 5514	1746 5523	1749 5532	1752 5541	1755 5550	1758 5559

Figure 20.3 European tabular writing: square roots.

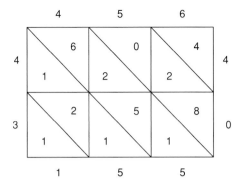

Figure 20.4 Lattice multiplication.

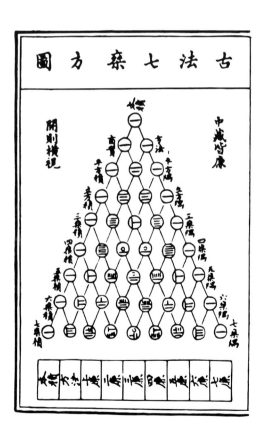

Figure 20.5 Chinese tabular writing.

sets of factors are seen as jointly co-determining the signification of an interrelated series of discrete forms.

Such a solution is unique to writing and there is no way it could be matched in speech. Here again the integrationist approach leads to the conclusion that the traditional reduction of writing to a 'representation' of speech lacks any theoretical credibility. If mathematics had had to rely on speech as its cognitive mode, we should still be living in a primitive agricultural society.

Chapter 21

Other forms of non-glottic writing

The potential range of non-glottic writing is infinite. That is to say, the variety of different activities which may be integrated through the use of written signs is unlimited. Human beings have so far exploited only a small proportion of these possibilities.

The present chapter considers three examples, selected to illustrate the ways in which glottic and non-glottic writing may be combined with other forms of graphic communication.

1 A commonly used type of knitting pattern combines two sets of instructions. One set takes a form such as:

> Using No. 3mm or 3¼mm needles and A cast on 37 [41:43:47:49:53:55: 59:61:65] sts.
> **1st Row**. – S1, k1, *p1, k1, rep from * to last st, k1.
> **2nd Row**. – S1, *p1, k1, rep from * to end.
> Rep 1st and 2nd rows 8 [8:9:9:10:10:10:11:11:11] times inc once at beg of last row for 24, 28, 32, 36, 40in or 61, 71, 81, 91, 102cm only. 38 [41:44:47:50:53:56:59:62:65] sts.
> Change to No. 3¾mm or 4mm needles and work 4 rows in st-st.
> Work from 1st to 26th row (inclusive) of Chart C once joining in and breaking off colours as required.
> The odd numbered rows are knit, the even numbered rows are purl.
> From 1st to 26th row (inclusive) of Chart C forms patt.[1]

The other set of instructions takes the form of a diagram (Fig 21.1).

The first set of instructions combines glottic with non-glottic writing. An example of the former is: 'The odd numbered rows are knit, the even numbered rows are purl.' An example of the latter is: 'S1, k1, *p1, k1' – which employs the special knitting symbols S, *p*, *k* and *. (The first three happen to be based on the English spelling of the words *slip*, *knit* and

---

1 Knitting pattern, Sirdar no. 6366.

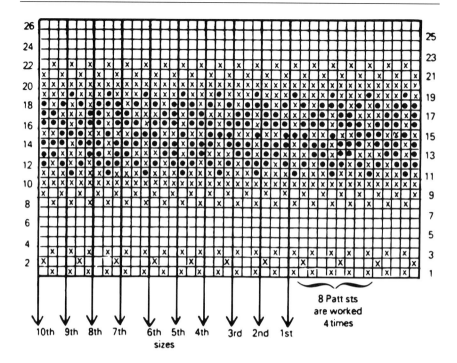

Figure 21.1 A mixed system.

purl; but this fact is not essential to their use as signs in knitting instructions.[2] The fourth – the asterisk – has no corresponding glottic basis.)

The second set of instructions (Fig. 21.1) exemplifies, in integrational terms, a 'mixed system' (Ch. 13). It has elements of a script (i.e. the symbols in the squares vary significantly in shape, corresponding to the different colours of wool used); but at the same time it requires the reader to adopt a scanning procedure which locates these symbols geometrically in a precisely mapped graphic space.

There is in principle no reason why *all* the information should not be presented in *either* form. In practice, this is not done because it would involve in one case a tediously long set of instructions, and in the other case a chart of such visual complexity as to be extremely difficult to 'read'.

The division of information as between the two modes of presentation relates to the integrational structure of the activities involved. It achieves the purpose of separating procedures that are easy to execute on the basis of inspecting an iconic configuration from those which require explanation

---

2   It should perhaps be pointed out that the use of an alphabet does not in itself make writing glottic. The International Phonetic Alphabet is an example of a non-glottic writing system applied to speech.

in terms of basic knitting concepts ('purl', 'slip', 'stocking stitch', etc.). Furthermore, the information handled in chart form relates to what is nearer to the terminal point of the whole operation (the configuration on paper can be mapped directly in visual terms on to the pattern of the finished garment), whereas the information handled in the first set of instructions is closer to the manipulative movements involved in the actual knitting.

The balance struck in the distribution of information in this example is probably close to the optimum. The point is that the optimum is determined by the nature of the activities to be integrated.

2 Dance notation is of particular interest from an integrational point of view, since it illustrates various aspects of complementarity between scriptorial and non-scriptorial signs.

In modern ballroom dancing diagrams, a commonly adopted convention is that the foot is represented by an outline of the sole of the shoe. For the right foot, this outline is filled in with dark hatching or shading, while for the left foot it is left blank (Fig. 21.2). The corresponding alphabetic forms are *RF* and *LF*.

Figure 21.2

When the foot swivels in making a turn, it may swivel either on the ball of the foot or on the heel. This is indicated diagrammatically by the position of a dotted outline, showing the sole of the foot in the position it has reached after the execution of the turn (Fig. 21.3). The corresponding alphabetic characters are *B* and *H*.

Figure 21.3

In dance manuals, however, we find that written instructions using conventional abbreviations are often accompanied by diagrams which make it unnecessary to give the full set of instructions in written form (Fig. 21.4).

Reverse Turn (Left Turn) followed by Left Closed Change

MAN

Begin facing diag. to centre   Music timing

1. Forward LF   1
2. Side RF   Turning to L   2 } 1 bar
                      to back LOD
3. Close LF to RF   3
4. Back RF   1
5. Side LF   2 } 1 bar
6. Close RF to LF   3

Finish facing diag. to wall.

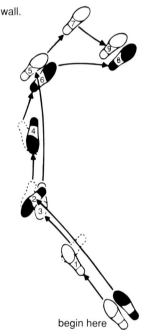

begin here

Figure 21.4

Thus in Figure 21.4 the written instructions for the waltz reverse turn do not mention explicitly that the man's first step turns with a swivel on the ball of the foot, but this is clear from the diagram. The instructions 'Begin facing diag. to centre' and 'Finish facing diag. to wall' are implicit in the diagram, since the convention is that the bottom-to-top dimension of the page indicates the 'line of dance', the left-hand side of the page the centre of the ballroom and the right-hand side the wall. A further unstated assumption is that the couples on a dance floor are proceeding in an anti-clockwise direction. Thus the external syntagmatics of the diagram is somewhat complex.

What the diagram does *not* include is the information relating to music timing – that is, that the first three steps occupy one bar, while the second three steps also occupy one bar. This is a major integrational difference between the written instructions and the diagram. That is to say, there is a further activity, which is actually essential to dancing a waltz, that finds no place in the diagram. This further activity is the co-ordination of the dance steps with the auditory rhythm of the accompanying music; and this is biomechanically quite a different task from the execution of the steps themselves. One might well be able to do the latter but not the former.

While the written instructions and the diagram can be read independently, they are interrelated both by the written phrase 'begin here' at the bottom of the diagram and by the numerals which appear in the diagram, corresponding to the numbered sequence of movements in the written instructions. (In the written instructions, the last three steps – the left closed change – are omitted, having been previously explained in the manual.)

The interesting feature of the instruction 'begin here' is that it can be read (i) as related externally to the ballroom floor, via the diagram, (ii) as related internally to the reading of the diagram itself, and (iii) as related externally to the sequence of written instructions given on the same page. Thus, in integrational terms, it is an example of syncretism, the single form fulfilling three distinct syntagmatic functions. It should be noted that all three are dependent on the position that the words *begin here* occupy in the graphic space provided by the diagram.

But this is not to be confused with cases of the type illustrated by Figure 21.5. Here, in Rameau's *Le maître à dancer* (1725) glottic forms are used non-glottically to give information about the orientation of the dancer in relation to the ballroom.

The example is theoretically of some importance, since it proves conclusively that there is no graphic disjunction between writing and diagram. It is different from cases in which the spiral form is used as a merely directional device, as presumably in the Phaistos disc (Fig. 21.6[3]) or

---

3   D. Diringer, *The Alphabet*, 2nd edn (London: Hutchinson, 1949), p. 78. This undeciphered text from Crete is cited in most histories of writing as a rare example of spiral writing at an early period. However, its authenticity has been called into question.

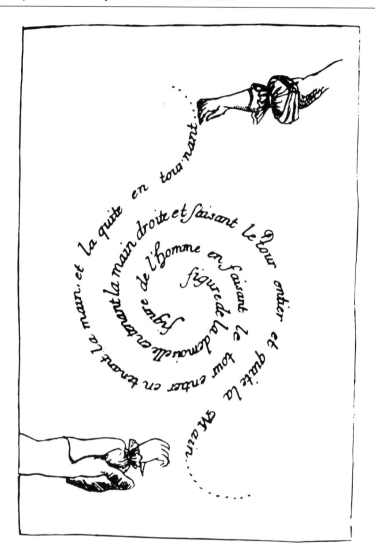

Figure 21.5 Non-glottic use of glottic forms.

Figure 21.6 Spiral writing: Phaistos disc.

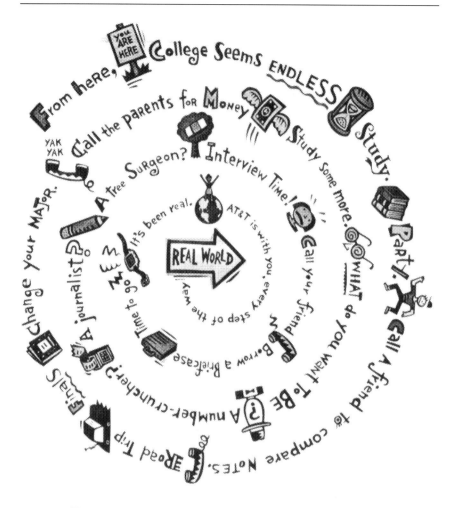

Figure 21.7 Spiral writing: AT & T advertisement, USA, 1993.

Figure 21.8 Labanotation.

whimsically in modern advertising (Fig. 21.7), precisely in that the internal syntagmatics of the writing also determines the pictorial interpretation of the diagram.

A system which dispenses with verbal instructions altogether is Labanotation.[4] In this system the equivalent of *begin here* is a double horizontal line, above which the first movement in question is indicated (Fig. 21.8).

Labanotation is based on a detailed analysis of body movements, relating the movements of specific parts of the body to spatial variables such as direction, level and distance and temporal variables such as speed, rhythm and duration. 'Textural' properties of the movement ('strong', 'heavy', 'elastic', etc.) may also be indicated. When, in addition, the path pattern of the dancer is shown, the resultant text reaches a level of visual complexity unknown in any other form of writing (Fig. 21.9).

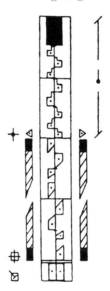

Figure 21.9 Labanotation.

Labanotation, from an integrational point of view, is a mixed system. Its use of the chart principle is directly geared to external syntagmatics, by reserving the left side of each symbol for information relevant to the left side of the body and the right side for information relevant to the right side of the body. (Compare this to the left–right division of bar code symbols (Fig. 13.2, p. 94), where the left side is – arbitrarily – reserved for

---

4   A. Hutchinson, *Labanotation*, 3rd rev. edn (New York: Routledge Theatre Arts, 1977).

information relating to the country and the manufacturer and the right for information relating to the product, plus a check digit.)

Labanotation provides a remarkable illustration of the power of writing. If we compare Labanotation with film as two means of recording dance, it becomes apparent that it would take several movie cameras filming simultaneously to cover all the points that a system of writing can deal with.[5]

3 Music writing falls into two basic types from an integrational point of view, although the difference between them is not necessarily evident from inspection of the text. But in both types, the notational units combine the functions of emblem and token.

Figure 21.10 shows a tenth-century Japanese score for flute music. The score is a tablature, i.e. the graphic characters relate directly to the fingering positions of a transverse flute, and not to the melody as such. In the West, although tablature scores for wind instruments are not unknown, it has been more usual for tablature writing to be used for stringed instruments, such as the lute and the guitar, and occasionally for keyboard instruments.[6] Otherwise the main tradition of notation has been directed towards recording the composition, not its execution.

The most striking feature of Western compositional writing is the development of the stave from the Middle Ages onwards. This system, unknown to the Greeks, who employed various literal notations, utilizes the graphic space available to separate out features of pitch from features of duration and succession. (From one point of view, this could be regarded as a compromise between compositional writing and tablature, since there is an obvious advantage to the player or singer who is sight-reading. But compositional writing does not indicate how variations of pitch are achieved.)

The reason for the development of the stave is readily explicable in integrational terms. It allows the reader a scanning strategy in which the relative height of a succession of notes provides a separate visual guide to the rise and fall of the melody. By comparison, any musical script in which each separate character has to indicate simultaneously pitch, duration and loudness would produce a musical text of less visual complexity but far greater difficulty from the performer's point of view.

5 *Ibid.*, pp. 7–8.
6 F. Dobbins, 'Tablature', in D. Arnold. (ed.), *The New Oxford Companion to Music*, vol. 2 (Oxford: Oxford University Press, 1983), pp. 1793–6.

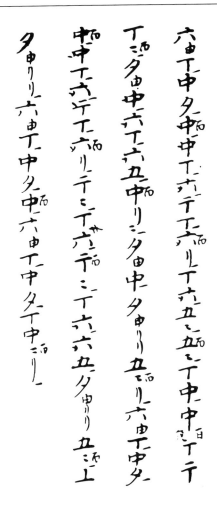

Figure 21.10 Japanese tablature.

Part V

Postscript

Chapter 22

Writing, context and culture

A semiological focus on writing both brings to attention and interrelates various aspects of the written sign which might otherwise be noted only by specialists in very disparate areas of study, such as calligraphy, graphology, advertising and esoteric symbolism.

Within an integrational framework, what such studies reveal can in many cases be recognized as patterns of signification which result from some specific contextualization of the written forms. These contextual factors may be of virtually any kind, ranging from the trivial and ephemeral to those involving the most deeply rooted of cultural beliefs.

An example of the latter: one is in no position to analyse the elaborate written forms found in certain Islamic manuscripts and inscriptions until one realizes that by far the most important text ever committed to writing in the Islamic world is the Koran. In a sense, the entire Islamic written tradition centres upon the preservation and propagation of this one text. Its sacrosanct nature precludes any possibility of allowing variations or reformulations that could be construed as altering 'the word' in any particular. But this leads naturally – and it is tempting to say inevitably – to embellishments of a formal nature in the scripts themselves. This is because, where copying the Koranic text is concerned, the dimensions of formal variation in letter shapes, layout, etc. are the only dimensions in which the signification of the written sign is not already subject to strict control. As Goody observes, 'the scribe can take no liberties with the verbal content of the Koran but is encouraged to elaborate complex patterns for the eye'.[1] This encouragement is all the greater in that, the text itself being already familiar to the faithful, there is no particular premium on legibility *per se*. Recognizability suffices. Thus the Basmalah turns up in virtually every graphic variant it would be possible to imagine over fourteen centuries of Islamic history.[2]

---

1 J. Goody, *The Domestication of the Savage Mind* (Cambridge: Cambridge University Press, 1977), p. 158.
2 Y.H. Safadi, *Islamic Calligraphy* (London: Thames & Hudson, 1978), pp. 32–9.

It would be a mistake to dismiss this proliferation of variations as merely 'decorative'. In fact, there is a double risk of error here. One is the risk of importing a Western concept of 'decoration' into cultural contexts where it may be quite misleading. (Even the term *calligraphy*, although commonly used in discussing the history of Islamic scripts, harbours potential misconceptions of this kind, inasmuch as the status and function of the Islamic calligrapher throughout history bear virtually no resemblance to those of the person nowadays described as practising calligraphy in the West.) The other is the risk of failing to see that the integration of the Islamic calligrapher's work into a tradition already laden with cultural values must *eo ipso* attract – at least for readers acquainted with that tradition – interpretations that assign significance to features in which the written forms continue or depart from those employed previously.

Furthermore, as students of Islamic writing have pointed out, the 'illegibility' of certain forms is not necessarily an undesired or undesirable effect. Commenting on the plaited Kufi of the famous profession of faith in Oljaitu's *mihrab* in the Friday mosque in Isfahan, which 'appears to the untutored eye merely as a network of arabesques', Annemarie Schimmel comments:

> This inscription has an almost magical character; indeed, one may understand it as a kind of amulet; for such inscriptions as this, illegible as they might appear, conveyed *baraka* to the onlooker. One is even inclined to say that, the more incomprehensible the text seemed, the more it radiated this quality of sacredness. . .[3]

A semiology of writing cannot afford to shrug all this off as being of no account, any more than a semiology of costume is entitled to dismiss in advance as irrelevant the introduction of variant forms of a garment.

In order to bring out the generality of the point being made here, it may be useful to compare the development of the myriad graphic variants of the Basmalah to the following case. A shop in Boston which provides photocopying services for students and others has a notice in the window which reads:

COPIES

not

COPIES.

The text as transcribed above is problematic, if not nonsensical. This is because what the transcription fails to reveal is that whereas the first word in the notice is printed crisply in black, the last word appears in characters of the same font, but less densely black and somewhat blurred. The distinction is visually subtle and requires a second glance to register – a requirement which makes the message all the more effective.

---

3   A. Schimmel, *Calligraphy and Islamic Culture* (London: Tauris, 1990), p. 10.

As in the case of Islamic calligraphy, we are dealing here with a cultural tradition in which graphic forms proliferate. To understand what this particular written text says, we have to see it as communicationally integrated into a world where your chances of impressing instructors, clients or potential employers are seen as possibly related to the quality of the photocopied material you submit for them to read. And recognizing the difference between a poor photocopy and a good one is part of the reading competence this culture assumes.

The contrast between the cases considered above shows that there is, in principle, no feature or features characteristic of written forms that might not, in the right cultural context, acquire a signification or even become the regular basis for new distinctions between written signs.

This is by far the most powerful reason for adopting an integrational approach to the semiology of writing. For whenever and wherever such a development occurs, and for whatever reason – i.e. when a new feature or set of features acquires significance in the formation of the written message – the semiological domain of writing is *eo ipso* extended. That is why any attempt to restrict the scope of semiological analysis by an *a priori* definition of writing must be rejected; for such a restriction fails to come to terms with the open-endedness of the very phenomenon it purports to investigate.

*   *   *

That open-endedness has been made ever more apparent since the advent of the computer. With its coming, all writing cultures entered a new era. For, as has been shrewdly observed, 'the distinction between reading and writing tends to disappear'.[4]

What does this mean in integrational terms? Essentially, what the computer has done is alter the concept of graphic space (Ch. 18). And it has done this by making possible feats of processing far in excess of human biomechanical limitations.

While it is true that readers have always been free to engage in 'selective reading' of a text, and in so doing have not – at least, in theory – been constrained by the structure of presentation embodied in the particular document in question, the cost of systematic selective reading, as measured by the human effort involved, has been high. One of the facilities the computer makes available is selective reading which eliminates this high cost. For the machine can undertake searches of the text and present the results with a speed and efficiency that far outstrip any human processing techniques.

The effect of this is that the graphic space occupied by an electronic text is not the static graphic space of the traditional document. It is a flexible

---

4 J.D. Bolter, 'Beyond word processing: the computer as a new writing space', *Language & Communication*, 8, 2/3 (1989), p. 130.

graphic space which the reader can shape and re-organize at will. Consequently, the internal syntagmatics of the text itself gains a new dimension. Repetitions, parallels, analogies and inconsistencies of which the writer may not have been aware at the time of composition can be – literally – brought into view by juxtaposition on the screen.

The writer, in turn, has corresponding options available which are not open in the composition of the traditional text. These include *refraining* from imposing any particular sequence on certain items or sections within it.

As the writer loses exclusive control of the graphic space and reading becomes a potential rewriting, the roles of writer and reader inevitably merge. The written text becomes a network of semiological possibilities to be negotiated between them.

At the same time, this negotiation depends on mechanical structures and programs over which both writer and reader have no direct control and about which, in typical cases, they are fairly ignorant. We can no longer see what happens when the finger presses the key, as we could in the days of the old manual typewriter.

* * *

In its role as writing-and-reading machine, however, the computer has the potential for bringing about an even greater revolution in human affairs.

Over the centuries, the traditional text has reflected and been constrained by the personal linguistic proficiency, experience and imagination acquired by individual writers and readers. The computer brings something new to this because it is a piece of equipment for speculative communicational engineering as well as simple recording. It can invent new words, new paradigms, new constructions, new languages if we wish. And it can access the contents of many libraries in order to do this. Thus its capacity for contextualization – and decontextualization – is many times greater than that of the most learned scholar.

What has gone virtually unnoticed is that a tool with this innovative power subverts received wisdom on the basic relationship between language, speech and writing. It erodes the distinction between verbal and non-verbal. It is a tool which already redefines our concept of the units of communication.

The word is no longer a static lexical unit belonging to an inventory established in a dictionary. For purposes of word-processing, the word can be any form or configuration that plays a role in the operations that develop a text. That role is not confined by the conventions or practices which govern the words of ordinary language. Nor is it restricted by the traditional boundary lines that deny word status to many classes of sign.

Here, in effect, we see alphabetization carried to its logical conclusion. Freed from speech altogether, the new superalphabet of the computer keyboard resolves writing into an array of characters in which forms as diverse as (i) **⋔**. , (ii) **#** , (iii) **⇨** , (iv) **⚷** and (v) **▭** can be conjured up at the touch of a key. Vowels and consonants are put on an equal footing with numerals, commas and dollars. The machine makes no distinction between them: it is a great leveller of signs.

Furthermore, new units and configurations of units can be invented as needed. The constraints on their invention are not constraints imposed from outside by the linguistic community, but constraints internal to the machine.

Do the modern superalphabets usher in a new concept of writing? Perhaps, after all, they merely allow us to see more clearly what writing always was.

Be that as it may, the new technology offers a form of communication which explodes the myth of writing as an ancillary recording system subservient to speech. It both vindicates the view of writing as a mode of communication *sui generis* and opens up a future in which writing is the essential, systematically creative process and speech merely oral commentary on what writing has created. That radical reversal of roles, we may reasonably speculate, will hold the key to the psychology of education in the next century.

Chapter 23

Writing and thought

Is writing in the end just a handy communication technology? Or are signs of writing signs of a distinctively human form of thought?

Such questions have been much discussed in recent years in the context of the debate over orality and literacy in human culture,[1] but the integrational theory of writing sketched in the preceding chapters throws new light on them. For what is at issue can be seen in a different perspective. This perspective enables one to disentangle such claims as 'writing restructures thought' and 'writing restructures consciousness'[2] from the scaffolding of confusions and question-begging assumptions by which they are all too frequently supported.

These assumptions include the notion that the primary function of writing is mnemonic, and that the alphabet, in virtue of its capacity to 'represent' speech economically, is superior to any pre-alphabetic system. From an integrational point of view, such assumptions lack any sound semiological basis.

The view that the Greeks were responsible for a quantum leap forward in human cognitive abilities by their introduction of alphabetic writing is particularly associated with Havelock:

> Atomism and the alphabet alike were theoretical constructs, manifestations of a capacity for abstract analysis, an ability to translate objects of perception into mental entities, which seems to have been one of the hallmarks of the way the Greek mind worked.[3]

According to Havelock's reconstruction of history, it would appear that by adding vowels to the consonant symbols borrowed from the Phoenicians,

---

1 See W.J. Ong, *Orality and Literacy* (London: Methuen, 1982) and the references contained therein; also, more recently, D.R. Olson and N. Torrance (eds), *Literacy and Orality* (Cambridge: Cambridge University Press, 1991).
2 Ong, *Orality and Literacy*, Ch. 4.
3 E.A. Havelock, *The Literate Revolution in Greece and its Cultural Consequences* (Princeton: Princeton University Press, 1982), p. 82.

the Greeks triggered a great release of psychic energy from which Western civilization still benefits.

> The alphabet, making available a visualized record which was complete, in place of an acoustic one, abolished the need for memorization and hence for rhythm. Rhythm had hitherto placed severe limitations upon the verbal arrangement of what might be said, or thought. More than that, the need to remember had used up a degree of brain-power – of psychic energy – which now was no longer needed. . . . The mental energies thus released, by this economy of memory, have probably been extensive, contributing to an immense expansion of knowledge available to the human mind.[4]

The degree of speculation in such claims is considerable. There is no historical evidence whatsoever that the alphabet was a 'theoretical construct' devised by any ancient Greek. If it was, then the theorizing involved had certainly been forgotten by the time of Plato, as the rambling discussion of letters in the *Cratylus* amply attests. No more plausible is the less ambitious claim sometimes advanced by linguists that the Greek alphabet shows that the Greeks achieved an 'unconscious phonemic analysis'.[5] What kind of cognitive feat an unconscious phonemic analysis might be is quite obscure, unless the phrase is no more than a circular redescription of the fact that the Greeks borrowed letter forms from another people and worked out a way of writing Greek with them. But that could hardly have been 'unconscious'. Furthermore, the supposition that the Greeks hit upon (what twentieth-century phonologists later called) the phonemic principle without realizing what they had done squares oddly with the account in which the alphabet is presented as a work of analytic genius. The phonemic principle is not the kind of thing it is possible to hit upon without realizing it, any more than to grasp the Newtonian law of gravitation without realizing it. (That is precisely why we attribute a grasp of that law to Newton, and not to his many predecessors in human history who had been struck on the head by falling apples but were none the wiser for it.)

Writing *qua* technology of communication, like all new technologies, was doubtless a mixed blessing in various respects. As Socrates was aware, it can be argued that the effect of reliance on writing will be not to liberate 'psychological space' but merely to weaken the memory. Furthermore, it is naive to assume that a reduction in the number of symbols used in a writing system automatically relieves the burden of memorization. Writing itself presumably imposes 'storage requirements' on the mind, and learning one's letters is not a simple matter of familiarizing oneself with a couple of dozen arbitrary shapes. Substitution of an alphabet for a syllabary, for all

---

4   *Ibid.*, p. 87.
5   R.H. Robins, *A Short History of Linguistics*, 2nd edn (London: Longman, 1979), p. 13.

we know, may well increase 'memory load' – if that is objectively measurable. If the reduction of the basic number of symbols were a criterion of efficiency, then clearly the binary system would be the optimum system of numerals. Significantly, only computers find this to be the case. Human beings don't.

Arguments based on historical half-truths and simplistic arithmetic do not take us very far towards addressing the questions raised by the claims mentioned above. If it is true that writing restructures thought, is that any more than a particular case of the more general truth that all new intellectual tools restructure thought? The question with every new intellectual tool is always: how does *this* innovation make possible or foster forms of thought which were previously difficult or impossible?

Any form of communication with the semiological properties that integrational analysis ascribes to writing might be expected, simply in virtue of having those properties, to promote one or more of the following:

1 the conceptualization of time in terms of spatial relations;
2 a progressive divorce between (written) history and oral tradition;
3 a divergence of recording functions between writing and pictorial and other iconic forms of representation;
4 the serious weakening or abolition of any equation between language and speech;
5 the conceptualization of the self as developing over time in ways amenable to documentation and retrospective evaluation;
6 the development of mathematics at an abstract level in advance of any pragmatic requirements of measurement;
7 the eventual recognition of an autonomous or 'timeless' status for the written form (regarded as having a 'permanent' or 'invariant' signification independent both of the writer and of the reader).

Now it cannot be argued that the historical association between the use of writing and any one or more of the above tendencies *of itself* demonstrates the consequences of writing on the way human beings think. But it cannot be denied either that any community which can draw upon some combination of them is *eo ipso* in possession of ways of making meaning that would find ready expression in some form of writing.

These seven tendencies are not ineluctable concomitants of the introduction of writing. There are always other factors in the cultural equation that determine to what extent, at particular times and places, they will become established and with what results. Furthermore, the observation that these tendencies occur at all – even sporadically – in the history of writing cultures can easily be dismissed by sceptics as a product of twenty–twenty hindsight. The fact remains that they do occur and seem to be directly related to the integrational potential of the written sign.

This potential, which spans activities and sensory modalities of the most diverse kinds, transforms the passage of time itself from a seemingly insuperable obstacle into a facilitating mechanism of human action. Thereby it transforms the way any individual with access to writing thinks about the possibility of interaction with all other individuals, past, present and future.

Appendix A

Notations as emblematic frames

Notations are based on a type of semiological structure found in many other forms of communication than writing; in particular in games, calendars, uniforms and rituals. Such structures may be termed *emblematic frames*.

The general characteristics of an emblematic frame may be described as follows.

1 Such a frame comprises a set of items (*emblems*), each of which has a distinctive form which identifies it as a member of the set. (Each item also usually has a name: e.g. the letter form σ is called *sigma*.)
2 Between any two items in the set, there is an equivalence relation or a relation of priority. Thus every item has a determinate 'position' in the set.
3 The number of items in the set is limited.
4 As a consequence of 1–3 above, each frame constitutes a structured system of which the members may be defined by their internal relationships to one another, independently of any functions each may acquire when the frame is integrated into ('used for') some specific set of communicational practices.

Examples:

A. The Japanese game of shenken is based on an emblematic frame comprising three emblems: Knife, Paper, Stone. The priorities are as follows: Knife takes priority over Paper, Paper over Stone, and Stone over Knife. The two players make a simultaneous choice of one of the three emblems. The winner is the player who has chosen the higher-ranking emblem.

It would be possible to imagine a different system of priorities using the same symbols; e.g. Knife takes priority over both Paper and Stone. This would still be an emblematic frame, but the three emblems would now be differently defined and the game, obviously, would lose its interest since players would always choose Knife.

B. In the standard Western pack of cards, each suit constitutes an emblematic frame (ace, king, queen, jack, ten, nine, etc.) and the pack comprises four such sets, each distinguished by a common symbol (heart, club, diamond, spade), plus a joker. The joker is an emblem which outranks all the others. In certain games, a deuce ranks above an ace. In others, priorities are assigned among the suits, or to one particular suit (trumps). Thus when the pack is integrated into a particular type of activity – e.g. the particular card game being played – relations between individual emblems may be suspended or overridden in accordance with a convention which is not part of the structure of the emblematic frame.

C. The Chinese calendar is based on the following emblems: Rat, Ox, Tiger, Rabbit, Dragon, Snake, Horse, Sheep, Monkey, Cock, Dog and Boar. The cycle is repeated every twelve years, always in the same order. But it can also be applied to other periods of time. Thus the system as such functions as an emblematic frame, with units defined simply by reference to the symbols and their order.

D. The standard gambling die constitutes an emblematic frame with a double structure, one being determined by the number of dots on each surface (one to six) and the other by the disposition of dots on the various faces of the cube (one opposite six, five opposite two, four opposite three). In different games or for divinatory purposes, different values are allotted to concurrent combinations of emblems which show when the dice are thrown and come to rest.

In the above examples, the emblematic frame has traditional origins associated with practices of specific kinds. But once the structure of the system has become established, it constitutes a semiological fact in its own right and can be used as the basis for other practices which have no necessary connexion with the traditional origins of the emblems in question.

This is the case with the alphabet, and is the reason why a set of alphabetic characters can be 'borrowed' without at the same time necessarily borrowing the phonological system originally associated with it.

A notation, in short, is simply an emblematic frame used for purposes of writing (in addition to any other purpose it may serve). The values associated with the emblems will vary according to the writing system in question.

Appendix B

Punctuation

The term *punctuation* is not well defined, in part because of long-running unresolved debates about the function of auxiliary marks employed in writing systems. It is not intended to enter in these debates here, but it should be noted that the term is used – by different scholars – to include marks with manifestly different functions, ranging from the commas and full stops of European alphabetic writing to the *matres lectionis* of Semitic texts.

From an integrational point of view, punctuation and other auxiliary marks fall into two main classes, depending on whether their presence in a text is due to activity on the part of the writer or the reader. In the latter case, they may be regarded as part of the processing of the text.

Until relatively recent times in China, this was the only kind of punctuation in regular use. The situation is summed up in the following terms by Viviane Alleton:

> Ancient texts were not punctuated. Any foreigner who has studied the old language remembers the discouragement of initial encounters with continuous texts in which there is no indication of sentence boundaries. One learns to spot where the sentences begin and end. A Chinese scholar will take pleasure in marking in his own hand the breaks or pauses in the text by putting small neat circles in red ink in the margins of his books. For the classical texts, where oral instruction played an important part, picking up the rhythm was doubtless easily learnt. In administrative, juridical and technical texts, stereotyped forms enabled readers to find their way.
>
> Punctuation was introduced only recently in China. In November 1919, teachers addressed a petition to the Ministry of Education urging the adoption of a system of punctuation along English lines. Today, linguistic and pedagogic periodicals and popular handbooks still devote much space to articles on the correct use of the punctuation marks.[1]

---

1 V. Alleton, *L'Ecriture chinoise*, 4th edn (Paris: Presses Universitaires de France, 1990), pp. 59–60.

In such a transition, clearly, the role of punctuation shifts, together with the responsibility for its use. Instead of being a processing device, it becomes part of the syntagmatic organization of the text.

The use of auxiliary marks as a reader's processing instrument is also common in the Western tradition.[2] It has taken a new form in recent times with the use of coloured 'highlighters' specially designed for the purpose of indicating words or sentences of particular interest to the individual reader.

The integrational function of punctuation in a quite different cultural context is confirmed by its development in ancient Egypt. Hieroglyphic texts have no punctuation, but punctuation marks appear in hieratic writing, particularly in poetry, and often written in red.[3] This way of including punctuation – but at the same time setting it apart from the text – seems to reflect recognition of its particular role in the processing needed for effective oral recitation.

Such a role is explicitly recognized for Greek in the *Techne grammatike* of Dionysius Thrax, where *anágnosis* (i.e. reading aloud) is treated as one of the six parts of grammar, and the function of the punctuation marks is clearly related to this. Reading aloud was not an easy exercise in the case of Greek, since texts were normally written without word division.[4]

Word division itself, although not always recognized as a form of punctuation in modern manuals (presumably because a blank space is not counted as a 'mark'), is one of the early aids to text processing supplied by the writer. It is in a sense 'built into' Chinese writing, since in most cases the individual character identifies a word. In Siamese, on the other hand, word spacing did not become usual until the introduction of the printing press in the nineteenth century.[5] In various ancient cuneiform systems of the Near and Middle East where polysyllabic words are common (including Ugaritic, Elamite and Old Persian) use of a word-divider is regularly in evidence. But in none of these cases is it taken as far as in Classical Tibetan, where syllable division, indicated by punctuation marks, becomes the organizing principle of the whole arrangement of characters (Ch. 9).

The earliest device of explicit syntagmatic separation, however, is the enclosure of groups of characters in boxes, which eventually leads to the systematic organization of the text in rows or columns (Ch. 18).

---

2 M.B. Parkes, *Pause and Effect. An Introduction to the History of Punctuation in the West* (Aldershot: Scolar, 1992), pp. 67–8.
3 H. Sottas and E. Drioton, *Introduction à l'étude des hiéroglyphes* (Paris: Geuthner, 1922; repr. 1991), p. 62.
4 See J. Lallot, *La Grammaire de Denys le Thrace* (Paris: CNRS, 1989), pp. 75–6.
5 D. Diringer, *The Alphabet*, 2nd edn (London: Hutchinson, 1949), p. 417.

Appendix C

Proto-writing

How writing may originally have been constructed on the basis of earlier sign systems is a question to which the integrationist can offer at least the outline of an answer. Sign systems in which marks were used as tokens and emblems would be the obvious precursors. Three such precursors have been discussed in recent publications.

Alexander Marshack has argued for the conclusion that already in the last Ice Age the ancestors of modern human beings were making attempts to establish a lunar calendar.[1] The method they devised for doing this was the incision of series of marks on suitable surfaces. (Marshack uses the term *notations* for these marks, but they are not notations in the sense defined in Ch. 15.)

If Marshack's interpretation is correct there is, in an integrationist perspective, a case for regarding these attempts as one beginning of a development which was to culminate eventually in the writing systems of later times. That is to say, no simple system of token-iterative recording (cf. the hypothetical sailor of Ch. 10) can develop into a calendar without exploiting the functional differentiation between token and emblem, which is the semiological foundation of writing.

Denise Schmandt-Besserat in numerous publications[2] has elaborated the thesis that in Mesopotamia records were kept from the ninth millennium onwards by means of collections of clay pellets of various shapes. (Schmandt-Besserat describes these as 'tokens', but her use of the term differs from that defined in Ch. 10.) Tracing the shapes of early Sumerian characters back to these pellets, she claims that they constitute a direct precursor of writing. If Schmandt-Besserat is right about the use of these pellets, they would also, from an integrational point of view, constitute a system based on the functional differentiation of emblem from token.

A third beginning can perhaps be detected in the evidence of Magda-

---

1 A. Marshack, *The Roots of Civilization*, rev. edn (Mt Kisco, NY: Moyer Bell, 1991).
2 Of these the most recent and comprehensive is D. Schmandt-Besserat, *Before Writing*, 2 vols (Austin: University of Texas Press, 1992).

lenian slates discussed by P.M. Russell.[3] The present writer has argued that these can be seen as recording devices providing the prototypes for synoptic reductions of the kind that are characteristically deployed in later systems of writing.[4] Here the marks would be tokens and the surface or object would have an emblematic function.

The essential difference between Marshack's 'calendars' on the one hand and Schmandt-Besserat's pellets and Russell's slates on the other is that the former enable their makers to impose a semiological structure on the passage of time by reference to a regular cycle of recurrent events, whereas the latter methods relate the passage of time adventitiously to an irregular sequence of events.

Such conjectures can be no more than speculative in our present state of knowledge. They nevertheless have a degree of plausibility which warrants calling such signs 'proto-writing'.

3   P.M. Russell, 'Plaques as paleolithic slates: an experiment to reproduce them', *Rock Art Research*, 6, 1 (1989), pp. 40–1, 68–9.
4   R. Harris, 'Writing and proto-writing: from sign to metasign', in G. Wolf (ed.), *New Departures in Linguistics* (New York: Garland, 1992).

Writing and analogy

The foundation of all writing is the human capacity to recognize and exploit analogies. Except in the fields of graphology and paleography, however, the systematic empirical study of analogy in writing has barely begun. Nevertheless, it may be helpful to propose some basic distinctions that need to be drawn.

1 *Biomechanical analogy*. The whole of graphology, in effect, is based on the fact that in handwriting individuals develop characteristic personal patterns of analogy in rhythm, letter formation and ligature that remain more or less stable over periods of time and which others are able to recognize. It is in fact difficult for mature adults to change or disguise their handwriting, even if they make deliberate attempts to do so. In other words, these patterns of analogy, once biomechanically automatized, are difficult to eradicate.

Handwriting experts study these graphic analogies mainly as signs of personal identity and 'character'. Other semiological aspects of the biomechanical phenomenon are less well studied: e.g. the maintenance of analogical features across a variety of circumstantial factors.

2 *Macrosocial analogy*. The essential difference between the concerns of the graphologist and those of the paleographer is that the latter focuses more upon patterns of analogy on the macrosocial scale, and seeks to characterize the similarities that go to make up a 'hand' or style of writing typical of a particular period, country, court, sect, scriptorium, etc.

Lettering and typographical design are related fields in which formal analogy plays a central role. The study of the alphabetic forms used in Caslon, Bodoni and other time-honoured styles shows a systematic effort to establish family resemblances, based on often subtle analogies of height, width, slant, weight, angularity, proportion, etc.

In modern commercial lettering (Fig. 1) this continues to be the case. Such analogies are instantly recognizable, even though no conscious effort is made to analyse them, and the average reader would probably be hard

Figure 1 Internal syntagmatics: analogical configuration.

put to it to point out exactly what graphic features create the impression of similarity.

However, of perhaps more general interest to the semiologist is the fact that, quite apart from the macrosocial development of styles of writing, all traditional writing systems exploit analogies internally as a means of syntagmatic articulation. Direction (Ch. 19) is nothing other than the systematic deployment of an analogical pattern connecting written characters. Familiarity with this pattern is what makes it possible for readers to take variations of alignment in their stride (Plate 19).

Chinese newspapers do not hesitate to combine horizontal and vertical writing on the same page. In Tokyo one sees taxis with the word TAXI written thus on one side of the vehicle but IXAT on the other, depending on the orientation of the written word with respect to the front of the vehicle (Plate 20). (In such cases the writing always follows the direction of the vehicle when travelling forward. Compare the similar phenomenon in Egyptian hieroglyphics, Fig. 19.1.) Presumably this variation would not be possible if people were unable to recognize the analogical pattern linking the two.

3 *Circumstantial analogy.* The use of colour[1] as a basis for circumstantial analogies is more or less ubiquitous in modern advertising. It is usually combined, however, with other methods. In Plate 4 at least three analogical patterns (based on colour, size and letter form) are used to articulate the internal syntagmatics of the text. Such analogies are also much employed as a means of linking physically separate graphic spaces. Thus in Plate 5 it is not immediately obvious what semiological role is played by the choice of colour scheme and open letter forms with shadowing; but this becomes clear as soon as the sign is seen in its context (Plate 6).

The importance of colour might perhaps be urged as a reason for treating

1 Colour in the sense in which human beings have colour vision, whereas many animals do not.

writing as an essentially visual mode of communication, as against the assumption adopted in the present study that in writing the basic formal relations are spatial. However, a study of the semiology of colour in written texts reveals that colour analogies are predominantly used as a means of emphasizing what is also articulated in terms of spatial relations, and rarely provide an independent dimension of signification. This is arguably one of the major semiological differences between writing and painting.

Bibliography

Alleton, V., (1990) *L'Ecriture chinoise*, 4th edn, Paris: Presses Universitaires de France.

Antonsen, E.H., (1989) 'The runes: the earliest Germanic writing system', in W.M. Senner (ed.), *The Origins of Writing*, Lincoln and London: University of Nebraska Press.

Arnheim, R., (1974) *Art and Visual Perception*, new edn, Berkeley: University of California Press.

Basso, K.H., (1974) 'The ethnography of writing', in R. Bauman and J. Sherzer (eds), *Explorations in the Ethnography of Speaking*, Cambridge: Cambridge University Press.

Beyer, S.V., (1992) *The Classical Tibetan Language*, Albany: State University of New York Press.

Blistène, B. *et al.*, (1993) *L'Ecriture de la danse*, Paris: Bibliothèque-Musée de l'Opéra.

Bolinger, D., (1946) 'Visual morphemes', *Language* 22, pp. 333–40.

Bolter, J.D., (1989) 'Beyond word processing: the computer as a new writing space', *Language & Communication*, 8, 2/3, pp. 129–42.

Boyer, C.B., (1991) *A History of Mathematics*, 2nd edn, New York: Wiley.

Buchler, J., (ed.) (1955) *Philosophical Writings of Peirce*, New York: Dover.

Burnet, J., (1948) *Early Greek Philosophy*, London: Black.

Cavanagh, A., (1955) *Lettering and Alphabets*, New York: Dover.

Chomsky, N. and M. Halle, (1968) *The Sound Pattern of English*, New York: Harper & Row.

Coe, M.D., (1992) *Breaking the Maya Code*, New York: Thames & Hudson.

Corbier, M., (1987) 'L'écriture dans l'espace publique romain', in *L'Urbs. Espace urbain et histoire*, Rome: Ecole française de Rome.

Coulmas, F., (1989) *Writing Systems of the World*, Oxford: Blackwell.

Crystal, D., (1992) *An Encyclopedic Dictionary of Language and Languages*, Oxford: Blackwell.

d'Alembert, J. le R., (1965) *Discours préliminaire de l'Encyclopédie*, Paris: Gonthier.

Davies, W.V., (1987) *Egyptian Hieroglyphs*, London: British Museum.

Derrida, J., (1974) *Of Grammatology*, trans. G.C. Spivak, Baltimore: Johns Hopkins University Press.

Diringer, D., (1949) *The Alphabet*, 2nd edn, London: Hutchinson.

Dobbins, F., (1983) 'Tablature', in D. Arnold (ed.), *The New Oxford Companion to Music*, vol. 2, Oxford: Oxford University Press.

Ernst, U., (1986) 'The figured poem: towards a definition of genre', *Visible Language*, xx, 1, pp. 8–27.

Folan, W.J., (1986) 'The calendrical and numerical systems of the Nootka', in M.P. Closs (ed.), *Native American Mathematics*, Austin: University of Texas Press.

Fraenkel, B., (1992) *La Signature. Genèse d'un signe*, Paris: Gallimard.

Franke, H., (1986) 'Chinese patterned texts', *Visible Language*, xx, 1, pp. 96–108.
Gelb, I.J., (1952) *A Study of Writing*, Chicago: University of Chicago Press; rev. edn 1963.
—— (1980) 'Principles of writing systems within the frame of visual communication', in P.A. Kolers, M.E. Wrolstad and H. Bouma (eds), *Processing of Visible Language*, vol. 2, New York: Plenum.
Goody, J., (1977) *The Domestication of the Savage Mind*, Cambridge: Cambridge University Press.
—— (1986) *The Logic of Writing and the Organization of Society*, Cambridge: Cambridge University Press.
Gusdorf, G., (1965) *Speaking*, trans. P.T. Brockelman, Evanston: Northwestern University Press.
Haas, W., (1983) 'Determining the level of a script', in F. Coulmas and K. Ehlich (eds), *Writing in Focus*, Berlin: Mouton.
Harris, R., (1981) *The Language Myth*, London: Duckworth.
—— (1983) (trans.) *F. de Saussure, Course in General Linguistics*, London: Duckworth.
—— (1986) *The Origin of Writing*, London: Duckworth.
—— (1987) *Reading Saussure*, London: Duckworth.
—— (1990) 'On redefining linguistics', in H.G. Davis and T.J. Taylor (eds), *Redefining Linguistics*, London and New York: Routledge.
—— (1992) 'Writing and proto-writing: from sign to metasign', in G. Wolf (ed.), *New Departures in Linguistics*, New York: Garland.
—— (1993) 'Three models of signification', in H.S. Gill (ed.), *Structures of Signification*, vol. III, New Delhi: Wiley.
—— (1994) *La Sémiologie de l'écriture*, Paris: CNRS.
Havelock, E.A., (1982) *The Literate Revolution in Greece and its Cultural Consequences*, Princeton: Princeton University Press.
Heath, T.L., (1921) *A History of Greek Mathematics*, Oxford: Clarendon Press.
Higgins, D., (1977) *George Herbert's Pattern Poems: In Their Tradition*, New York: Unpublished Editions.
Hofman, H., (1978) 'Sator-quadrat', in Pauly/Wissowa (eds), *Realencyclopädie*, suppl. vol. 15, Munich: Druckenmüller.
Holenstein, E., (1983) 'Double articulation in writing', in F. Coulmas and K. Ehlich (eds), *Writing in Focus*, Berlin: Mouton.
Houston, S.D., (1989) *Maya Glyphs*, London: British Museum.
Hutchinson, A., (1977) *Labanotation*, 3rd rev. edn, New York: Routledge Theatre Arts.
Keightley, D.N., (1978) *Sources of Shang History: The Oracle-Bone Inscriptions of Bronze Age China*, Berkeley: University of California Press.
Komatsu, E. and R. Harris, (eds) (1993) *F. de Saussure, Troisième cours de linguistique générale (1910–1911)*, Oxford: Pergamon.
Kroeber, A.L., (1923) *Anthropology*, New York: Harcourt, Brace.
Lallot, J., (1989) *La Grammaire de Denys le Thrace*, Paris: CNRS.
Lévi-Strauss, C., (1973) *Tristes Tropiques*, trans. J. Weightman and D. Weightman, London: Cape.
Long, J., (1987) *The Art of Chinese Calligraphy*, Poole: Blandford.
Luria, A.R., (1978) 'The development of writing in the child', in M. Cole (ed.), *The Selected Writings of A.R. Luria*, White Plains, NY: Sharpe.
Mallery, G., (1893) *Picture-Writing of the American Indians*, Washington: Government Printing Office; repr. New York: Dover, 1972.
Marcus, J., (1992) *Mesoamerican Writing Systems*, Princeton, NJ: Princeton University Press.

Marett, A.J., (1977) 'Tunes notated in flute-tablature from a Japanese source of the tenth century', *Musica Asiatica* I, pp. 1–60.

Marshack, A., (1991) *The Roots of Civilization*, rev. edn, Mt Kisco, NY: Moyer Bell.

Martlew, M., (1983) 'The development of writing: communication and cognition', in F. Coulmas and K. Ehlich (eds), *Writing in Focus*, Berlin, New York and Amsterdam: Mouton.

Miller, J., (1971) *McLuhan*, London: Fontana/Collins.

Miller, J.C.P. and F.C. Powell, (1965) *The Cambridge Elementary Mathematical Tables*, Cambridge: Cambridge University Press.

Mintz, P.B., (1981) *Dictionary of Graphic Art Terms*, New York: Van Nostrand Reinhold.

Neugebauer, O., (1957) *The Exact Sciences in Antiquity*, 2nd edn, Providence: Brown University Press.

Olson, D.R. and N. Torrance (eds) (1991) *Literacy and Orality*, Cambridge: Cambridge University Press.

Ong, W.J., (1982) *Orality and Literacy*, London: Methuen.

Orwell, G., (1949) *Nineteen Eighty-Four*, London: Secker & Warburg; repr. 1987, Harmondsworth: Penguin.

Page, R.I., (1987) *Runes*, London: British Museum.

Parkes, M.B., (1992) *Pause and Effect. An Introduction to the History of Punctuation in the West*, Aldershot: Scolar.

Peirce, C.S., (1931–1958) *The Collected Papers of Charles Sanders Peirce*, vols I–VI, ed. C. Hartshorne and P. Weiss; vols VII–VIII, ed. A. Burks, Cambridge, Mass.: Harvard University Press.

Pettersson, J.S., (1991) *Critique of Evolutionary Accounts of Writing* (RUUL No. 21), Uppsala: Department of Linguistics, Uppsala University.

Pope, M., (1975) *The Story of Decipherment*, London: Thames & Hudson.

Powell, M.A. Jr, (1972) 'The origin of the sexagesimal system: the interaction of language and writing', *Visible Language*, VI, 1, pp. 5–18.

Pulgram, E., (1976) 'The typologies of writing-systems', in W. Haas (ed.), *Writing Without Letters*, Manchester: Manchester University Press.

Rouse, R.H. and M.A. Rouse, (1989) 'Wax tablets', *Language & Communication*, 9, 2/3, pp. 175–91.

Russell, P.M., (1989) 'Plaques as paleolithic slates: an experiment to reproduce them', *Rock Art Research*, 6, 1, pp. 40–1, 68–9.

Safadi, Y.H., (1978) *Islamic Calligraphy*, London: Thames & Hudson.

Sampson, G., (1985) *Writing Systems*, London: Hutchinson.

Saussure, F. de, (1922) *Cours de linguistique générale*, 2nd edn, Paris: Payot.

Schimmel, A., (1990) *Calligraphy and Islamic Culture*, London: Tauris.

Schmandt-Besserat, D., (1992) *Before Writing*, 2 vols, Austin: University of Texas Press.

Silvester, V., (1993) *Modern Ballroom Dancing*, rev. edn, North Pomfret: Trafalgar Square.

Smalley, W.A., C.K. Vang and G.Y. Yang (1990) *Mother of Writing. The Origin and Development of a Hmong Messianic Script*, Chicago: University of Chicago Press.

Sottas, H. and E. Drioton, (1922) *Introduction à l'étude des hiéroglyphes*, Paris: Geuthner, repr. 1991.

The Highway Code, rev. edn (1987), London: HMSO.

Thomas, I., (1939) *Greek Mathematical Works*, vol. 1, Cambridge, Mass.: Harvard University Press; London: Heinemann (Loeb Classical Library).

Trager, G.L., (1974) 'Writing and writing systems', in T.A. Sebeok (ed.), *Current Trends in Linguistics*, vol. 12, The Hague and Paris: Mouton.

Tylor, E.B., (1881) *Anthropology*, London: Macmillan.

Vachek, J., (1948) 'Written language and printed language', *Recueil linguistique de*

Bratislava, pp. 67–75; repr. in J. Vachek (ed.), *A Prague School Reader in Linguistics*, Bloomington: Indiana University Press, 1964.

van Ginneken, J., (1939) 'Die Bilderschrift-Sprachen', *Travaux du Cercle Linguistique de Prague*, 8, pp. 247–55.

—— (1940) 'La reconstruction typologique des langues archaïques de l'humanité', *Verhandelingen der K. Nederlandsche Akademie van Wetenschappen* (Letterkunde, NR xliv), Amsterdam.

Walker, C.B.F., (1987) *Cuneiform*, London: British Museum.

Wilkins, J., (1694) *Mercury: or the Secret and Swift Messenger*, 2nd edn, London.

Index